Innovation and Structural Transformation in Asia

This book explores recent drivers of Asia's growth and economic development. The analysis is based on a database created by the authors. It covers a large number of economies, including 39 from Asia for the period 1990–2020.

The database and the analysis in the book use novel indicators of development. It is structured along four areas: productivity and structural change, global value chains (GVCs), economic complexity, and the Fourth Industrial Revolution (4IR). The book offers insights into current economic performance and future prospects. It shows great heterogeneity across the region, highlighting a range of development experiences. Each chapter contains an accessible methodological section of the concepts used, explaining the construction of indicators and how they should be interpreted.

The book will interest scholars of Asian economics, structural transformation, productivity, GVCs, complexity, and 4IR studies. The publicly available database will also appeal to policymakers and researchers interested in data analysis.

Jesus Felipe is a Distinguished Professor of Economics at De La Salle University (The Philippines). His research on growth and structural transformation has been published in the *Cambridge Journal of Economics*, *Journal of Comparative Economics*, *Journal of Evolutionary Economics*, *Structural Change and Economic Dynamics*, and *World Development*.

Neil Foster-McGregor is a Senior Economist at the Asian Development Bank. His research on growth, trade, and structural transformation has been published in *Industrial and Corporate Change*, *Research Policy*, *Structural Change and Economic*, and *World Development*.

Önder Nomaler is a Senior Researcher at UNU-MERIT (The Netherlands). His research on evolutionary economics has been published in *Research Policy*, *Structural Change and Economic Dynamics*, *Economics of Innovation and New Technologies*, *Journal of Evolutionary Economics*, and the *Journal of Economic Geography*.

Bart Verspagen is a Professor of the Macroeconomics of Innovation and New Technology at Maastricht University (The Netherlands). He has published extensively in the field of innovation research and is editor of *Journal of Evolutionary Economics*. He holds an honorary doctorate from the University of Oslo.

Innovation and Structural Transformation in Asia

Jesus Felipe, Neil Foster-McGregor, Önder Nomaler, and Bart Verspagen

LONDON AND NEW YORK

First published 2025
by Routledge
4 Park Square, Milton Park, Abingdon, Oxon OX14 4RN

and by Routledge
605 Third Avenue, New York, NY 10158

Routledge is an imprint of the Taylor & Francis Group, an informa business

© 2025 Jesus Felipe, Neil Foster-McGregor, Önder Nomaler, and Bart Verspagen

The right of Jesus Felipe, Neil Foster-McGregor, Önder Nomaler, and Bart Verspagen to be identified as authors of this work has been asserted in accordance with sections 77 and 78 of the Copyright, Designs and Patents Act 1988.

All rights reserved. No part of this book may be reprinted or reproduced or utilised in any form or by any electronic, mechanical, or other means, now known or hereafter invented, including photocopying and recording, or in any information storage or retrieval system, without permission in writing from the publishers.

Trademark notice: Product or corporate names may be trademarks or registered trademarks, and are used only for identification and explanation without intent to infringe.

British Library Cataloguing-in-Publication Data
A catalogue record for this book is available from the British Library

ISBN: 978-1-032-96662-5 (hbk)
ISBN: 978-1-032-96664-9 (pbk)
ISBN: 978-1-003-59033-0 (ebk)

DOI: 10.4324/9781003590330

Typeset in Times New Roman
by KnowledgeWorks Global Ltd.

Contents

Access to the Database		*vi*
Preface		*vii*
1	Innovation and Structural Transformation in Asia	1
2	Introduction to Asia's Development	16
3	Labor Productivity and Structural Transformation in Asia	27
4	Recent Developments in Global Value Chains in Asia	40
5	Economic Complexity in Global Value Chains in Asia	62
6	The Fourth Industrial Revolution Technologies in Asia	79
7	Conclusions: Moderate Optimism About Asia's Development Prospects	90
	References	*95*
	Index	*101*

Access to the Database

Please access the database at: https://dataverse.nl/dataverse/innovation_and_ structural_transformation_database

Preface

This book came as an idea years ago when we thought of working on a database that contained a novel dataset to analyze development. This dataset should contain indicators of development different from those traditionally used, and not readily available. This obeys to our understanding of development as a process that combines structural transformation and the accumulation of capabilities at the firm level.

The database also contains indicators of complexity. Work in this area has been developed during the last two decades, and it has also influenced our work and thinking. This work links with the old classical structural transformation school. It has developed very useful metrics (allowed by the availability of large datasets on trade) that permit a more detailed understanding of development.

We have also been influenced for quite some time by the discussions about the importance and implications of global value chains (GVCs). Whether GVCs are a development escalator (if countries move to the most complex stages of the chain) or a hindrance to development (because many developing countries find it very difficult to move up), the reality is that during the last decades, GVCs have become fundamental mechanisms of production and trade. We thought it important to document how countries are integrated into them.

Finally, the recent discussions about the possibilities offered by the technologies that make up the Fourth Industrial Revolution led us to develop a section on these technologies because, some argue, they offer windows of opportunities to leapfrog.

We have made an effort to write an accessible book that can be used by development practitioners and students. Our interest is in Asia, but data for other countries can equally be downloaded and studied. Possibly, as it happens with most first editions of books, this one will not meet everyone's expectations. We hope to correct this in the future. We welcome feedback.

We are indebted to Cristina Sevilla, Jesus Felipe's Assistant at De La Salle University, for her excellent work putting together the entire manuscript, formatting it, and making sure that it "looks good."

Jesus Felipe, Manila
Neil Foster-McGregor, Manila
Önder Nomaler, Maastricht
Bart Verspagen, Maastricht
November 2024

1 Innovation and Structural Transformation in Asia

1.1 Overview of Book

This book uses information from a unique database, the Innovation and Structural Transformation Database, created by the authors, to study development. It can be accessed at: https://dataverse.nl/dataverse/innovation_and_ structural_transformation_database/ (Foster-McGregor et al. 2024a, 2024b). This database contains information (indicators) for a large number of countries across the world, including a broad range of Asian economies at all levels of development, about the following four areas: (i) productivity and structural change (Chapter 3), (ii) global value chains (Chapter 4), (iii) economic complexity in global value chains (Chapter 5), and (iv) the Fourth Industrial Revolution (4IR) (Chapter 6). The appendix to this chapter provides a detailed description of the files in the database and all the indicators available.

The time-series coverage depends on the specific indicators, but generally the range is 1990–2020. The four dimensions are key areas needed to assess countries' performance, and from there infer how they will do in what remains of the 21st century.

The focus of the book is Asia because this is our research interest. The region is highly dynamic and highly integrated globally, yet, at the same time, it is highly heterogeneous. One important aspect of the book is that it highlights this heterogeneity in terms of major drivers of long-run growth. We extracted the values of the indicators for 39 Asian economies – the information available about each of them varies – and analyzed them. These economies are Afghanistan, Armenia, Azerbaijan, Bangladesh, Bhutan, Brunei Darussalam, Cambodia, Fiji, Georgia, Hong Kong, India, Indonesia, Japan, Kazakhstan, Kyrgyz Republic, Lao PDR, Myanmar, Malaysia, Maldives, Mongolia, Nepal, Pakistan, Papua New Guinea, People's Republic of China (China hereafter), the Philippines, Samoa, Solomon Islands, Singapore, South Korea, Sri Lanka, Taiwan, Tajikistan, Thailand, Timor-Leste, Tonga, Turkmenistan, Uzbekistan, Vanuatu, and Vietnam. We note that we use the terms "country" and "economy" indistinctly. We encourage researchers to use the database and explore other economies.

A summary of the analysis is as follows.

DOI: 10.4324/9781003590330-1

1.1.1 Chapter 2: Introduction to Asia's Development

The fundamental drivers of Asia's long-run growth and development have been a source of discussion since the early 1990s. Although East Asia's growth (starting with Japan) had been documented earlier, the discussion has taken a different direction since the 1990s. A group of economists used the neoclassical growth model to decompose output growth into the contributions of labor and capital growth, and that of total factor productivity growth, for Hong Kong, Singapore, South Korea, and Taiwan, for the period between the mid-1960s and the early 1990s (Young 1992, 1994, 1995; Kim and Lau 1994). These authors reached the surprising result that the contribution of total factor productivity growth was very small, virtually zero in the case of Singapore.

This result gave rise to a very important debate in the profession: could it be true that the growth rates registered by these economies during the said period, 7%–10% per annum, as well as the significant change in export composition, could have been attained without productivity growth, or technical progress?

Indeed, a different group of economists argued that the neoclassical growth model could not explain the essence of East Asia's high growth, namely, the phenomenal transformation of these economies, together with the increase in firms' capabilities. The role of the state was also fundamental (Amsden 1989, 1995; Wade 1990; Stiglitz 1996; Nelson and Pack 1999), something questioned by orthodox economists. Felipe and McCombie (2003) offered a methodological critique of the neoclassical growth accounting approach.

Understanding how these economies achieved these growth rates became a subject of research in the 1990s. Did the profession have models that could explain such a unique experience? Could other countries follow their steps? The answers to these questions turned out to be one of the most interesting debates in the profession, namely, that of East Asia's sources of (high) growth. Felipe et al. (2025) provide a survey of this debate.

Although the debate (like others in economics) died during the following two decades without a clear answer, growth and development pundits have continued discussing Asia's growth (more broadly) until today. The reason is that while the debate about the four East Asian economies continued, another Asian economy, China, made headlines. Some economists used the same neoclassical approach to understand China, and the same debate ensued. Other Asian economies have attained fast growth rates of output (6% and above) recently and have also drawn attention. These include India, the Philippines, and Vietnam: how have they done it?

The background of this book is the authors' belief that Asia's development cannot be explained adequately by the neoclassical model (growth accounting exercises). Instead, and following Felipe et al. (2025), we argue that it is best explained by bringing into the discussion the significant structural transformation that these economies underwent, and many are still undergoing. It also requires analysis of the substantial upgrading of their export structures, increase in firms' capabilities, and the role of the government facilitating and encouraging structural transformation through different tools of industrial policy. We also provide a macroeconomic perspective of how the East Asian economies managed to attain such high growth rates without running into balance of payments problems.

Moreover, recent decades have seen the rise of new potential forces of development. These include the increasing role of global value chains (GVCs) as a development tool and the rise of new digital technologies that represent both an opportunity and a threat to development. Along with these changes, there has been important new work in the measurement and analysis of economic development and its drivers, including the use of multi-region input-output tables and network methods. This book focuses on these new sources.

1.1.2 Chapter 3: Labor Productivity and Structural Change in Asia

This chapter analyzes labor productivity in Asia, both the level and its growth rate. Labor productivity varies significantly across the Asian economies. Yet, there has been convergence in labor productivity, that is, economies whose labor productivity was lower in 2000 registered higher growth rates during 2000–2019. We also observe a strong positive association between the growth rate of manufacturing labor productivity and aggregate labor productivity growth.

A decomposition of labor productivity growth into within-sector productivity growth and inter-sectoral productivity growth, or structural change (divided into a dynamic component, that is, a movement of labor toward sectors that had relatively high labor productivity growth rates over the period under consideration; and a static component, that is, a movement of labor toward sectors that had an initially high level of labor productivity), indicates that for most economies, most of labor productivity growth is accounted for by the within-sector component, with agriculture, manufacturing, and other activities accounting for the majority of the within effect. Growth due to structural change played a smaller role. This component was nevertheless relatively important for economies such as Lao PDR, Cambodia, Bangladesh, Papua New Guinea, Indonesia, and Vietnam, among others, particularly the static structural change term. The dynamic structural change term played a positive role in just a few economies, notably Myanmar, China, Georgia, and Lao PDR. Labor in many

4 *Innovation and Structural Transformation in Asia*

Asian economies has shifted out of agriculture toward construction and certain services sectors, such as trade, transport, and other activities. Conversely, there has – on average – been little shift toward manufacturing in recent years, which raises concerns around the long-run development impacts of a lack of industrialization.

1.1.3 Chapter 4: Recent Developments in Global Value Chains in Asia

GVCs are commonly seen as a vehicle for economic development, allowing economies to integrate into the global economy and to industrialize by specializing in certain activities within a product's value chain. Concerns remain, however, regarding the ability of developing economies to extract significant value added from the value chain and to upgrade within value chains. Such concerns relate to the positioning of economies within value chains, including the sectors in which economies contribute as well as their positioning within sectors (e.g., whether they are final assemblers or whether they provide significant value added to other economies' value chains). Recently, questions have been raised about the stagnation of global value chains and whether value chains are becoming increasingly regional rather than global.

The Innovation and Structural Transformation Database uses data from the Asian Development Bank's multi-country input output tables and includes information on selected GVC indicators for 64 economies (including a rest-of-the-world category).[1]

The analysis provides evidence to suggest that overall GVC integration of the Asian countries increased over time (2007–2019), though this hides a great deal of heterogeneity. Some economies have withdrawn from GVCs, while others have expanded their levels of integration. These developments have further been driven by changes in the relative positioning of economies and sectors within GVCs. At the extremes are China and Vietnam, with the former witnessing declining GVC integration through both forward and backward integration and the latter observing increasing GVC integration. Despite this, both economies have been able to increase their share of world value added in global exports.

A more consistent picture emerges when considering the geographical dimension of GVC developments. For most Asian economies, a movement toward a more regional bias to GVC integration is observed, suggesting a regionalization of value chains in the region. An exception to this pattern is China, which has seen a slight movement toward more global integration through value chains, both in terms of its sourcing patterns and the value added that is provided to other economies.

1.1.4 Chapter 5: Economic Complexity in Global Value Chains in Asia

The complexity of an economy reflects the number and kinds of products that it can export successfully, with higher levels of complexity linked to improved economic growth and development. The Innovation and Structural Transformation Database combines information on complexity with information on GVC integration. This permits us to define indicators about the complexity of the inputs that are part of the production process and the complexity of final output for a variety of sectors. Using these data, we examine two issues: first, the relationship between the complexity of inputs into the production process and the complexity of the resulting output, with a focus on the complexity of foreign inputs and two GVC sectors, electrical and optical equipment, and textiles; second, the relationship between the complexity of foreign inputs and that of output and the extent of GVC integration. We focus on whether deeper GVC integration is a driver of, or a consequence of, improvements in the complexity of production.

The analysis provides evidence to suggest that there is a positive association between domestic and foreign input complexity, indicating that they are somewhat complementary, particularly in the case of textiles. Asian economies have also been able to upgrade the complexity of their final output over time. In the case of electrical and optical equipment, improvements in final output complexity are often found to occur in combination with improvements in foreign input complexity – suggesting an important role for foreign inputs in upgrading opportunities in final production for these economies in electricals. In the case of textiles, however, the improvement in final output complexity is often found to occur despite a decline in foreign input complexity – suggesting an important role for domestic input complexity in driving final output complexity.

Despite the observed relationship between input and output complexity, there is little association between the extent of complexity upgrading – on both the input and output side – and GVC integration. Deeper integration in GVCs can be accompanied by increases or decreases in foreign input complexity and increases or decreases in final output complexity, suggesting that enhanced integration in GVCs does not guarantee upgrading.

1.1.5 Chapter 6: The Fourth Industrial Revolution Technologies in Asia

The 4IR has raised expectations about significant changes in the way we live, work, and interact, even more so than those created by the technologies associated with the Second Industrial Revolution (electricity, telephone, automobile). This has to do with the potential that the new technologies have to create

General-Purpose Technologies that truly change our life. These technologies include robotics, additive manufacturing, artificial intelligence, the internet of things, and big data.

It is likely that these technologies will have both positive (e.g., increase income levels) and negative (e.g., disrupt employment in the short run) impacts. The latter raises the concern that economies that are not engaged in the production or use of 4IR technologies may miss out on some of the major gains from the 4IR, perpetuating existing income disparities and further exacerbating cross-economy inequality. Economies that are not engaged in innovative activity within 4IR may still benefit from the technologies if they either produce and export products that embody 4IR technologies or if they import and use such products in their production process.

The involvement in 4IR innovation by the Asian economies is highly concentrated in a few developed and emerging economies (e.g., Japan, China, South Korea). The majority of Asian economies, therefore, are not involved at all in patenting in 4IR technologies. This is true for some relatively fast-growing economies, such as Thailand. Such results raise concerns that even within Asia, there may be divergent effects of the 4IR, with a small number of economies active in the production of 4IR technology and likely to benefit from innovation in this area, and a majority of economies excluded from such innovative activity.

These concerns are exacerbated by the observation that most Asian economies do not have comparative advantage in either the export or import of 4IR technologies, suggesting that they are currently largely excluded from the 4IR. Conversely, the Asian economies that account for the majority of 4IR patents are also the economies that tend to have a comparative advantage in both the export and import of 4IR products. This calls for a word of caution: this assessment, based on patents, does not imply that there is no innovation whatsoever in Asia's laggard economies. Indeed, the innovation landscape is very vibrant if one does not confine the analysis to standard measures of innovation (Fu and Shi 2022). These nations undertake significant amounts of "intermediate innovations" (what the literature also refers to as behind-the-frontier catch up) to adapt imported technologies to their context (i.e., product processes). We do not consider this type of innovation.

1.1.6 Chapter 7: Conclusions: Moderate Optimism about Asia's Development Prospects

Asia is a very heterogeneous region. Our analysis based on the indicators of labor productivity and structural transformation, global value chains, complexity, and the 4IR, indicates that China, Hong Kong, Japan, Singapore, South Korea, and Taiwan progressed a great deal during the second part of the 20th century and the first quarter of this century. Their economies have undergone significant transformation and have become more complex; they are engaged in global value chains; and they participate in the creation of the technologies that constitute the 4IR technologies. Most other Asian countries do not score as well. Malaysia and Thailand have also undergone significant structural transformation, with the former approaching high income, but both are behind in the generation of the technologies of the 4IR.

The rest is far behind in several indicators. Progress for these economies in the rest of this century will be a slow process. While some of them will get closer to the advanced economies (e.g., Indonesia, the Philippines) due to their higher growth rates, they will still trail behind. For example, the structural transformation of these economies is towards high employment shares in low productivity services, not manufacturing. Also, R&D in the technologies of the 4IR is almost nonexistent.

Appendix: The Innovation and Structural Transformation Database

The database on which the empirical analysis in this book is built contains four main pillars, each with its own indicators: (1) Labor Productivity and Structural change, (2) Global Value Chains, (3) Product Complexity, and (4) Innovation. In the database, each of these pillars contains two sub-pillars in the form of an Excel file with the indicators. Here, we describe each pillar and provide the full list of indicators available in Table A1. Details are provided by Foster-McGregor et al. (2024b).

Labor Productivity and Structural Change

This pillar contains information on the sectoral structure of the economy and its changes, productivity, and the way in which structural change interacts with productivity change. It also contains data on international trade in products related to new technology (so-called 4IR products).

The file *DB_Structural_Change_Basic_Indicators.xlsx* contains data on the sectoral structure of the economy (value added, household consumption and total demand, including government consumption and private investment); the structure of exports and imports as classified by their use in global value chains (e.g., intermediate good, capital goods, consumer goods); and the value of imports and exports in specific products related to the 4IR.

In *DB_Structural_Change_ProductivityGrowth.xlsx*, data on the structural decomposition of productivity growth can be found, as well as the decompositions themselves. This file contains data on employment, value added and productivity growth, relative labor productivity between sectors, and shares of value added and employment, all for a variety of sectors within national economies. Finally, the file also contains the decompositions of productivity growth over various periods.

Global Value Chains

This pillar has indicators on sector-level GVC integration of countries. This includes forward (to which GVC's value added is directed) and backward (from which sectors GVC value originates) perspectives. A regional (in terms of global regions) perspective on GVCs is also provided.

In the file *DB_GVC_Integration.xlsx*, the basic GVC indicators are presented. This includes the various parts (own sector, other domestic sectors, and foreign) of forward and backward integration, both in terms of shares and specialization indices.

The file *DB_GVC_Radius.xlsx* presents indicators on regionalization of GVCs. These are distance-based indicators of forward and backward integration.

Product Complexity

This pillar contains data on upgrading opportunities in international trade. Product complexity is used as the basic indicator, and this is applied to analyzing upgrading opportunities at the detailed product level for exports, as well as in the context of GVCs at a more aggregated sectoral level.

Data on complexity in GVCs are in the file *DB_Input_And_Output_Complexities.xlsx*. The indicators in this file use the GVC perspective, based on input-output tables, that is also used in the Innovation pillar of the database. They represent the average complexity of products at various stages of the GVC.

The file *DB_Upgrading_Capabilities.xlsx* contains data on upgrading possibilities in terms of gross exports. This follows a related diversity approach, where countries' upgrading possibilities are evaluated in terms of the complexity of "target products" and their relatedness to the country's existing specialization profile.

Innovation

This pillar of the database has information on patenting in 4IR technologies, by country and technology group. It also applies these technology indicators to the GVC indicators by calculating 4IR patenting intensity of various stages of the GVC.

The file *DB_IR4patents_2000_2019.xlsx* contains indicators on patenting, such as a count of the number of patent families in each 4IR subgroup and the share of groups in total patents per country. These counts are done per year, and for 10-year cumulative periods. Counts for all technologies are provided for comparison.

The file *DB_Patents_Embedded_in_GVCs.xlsx* combines patent indicators with GVC indicators to create indicators for the technology content of GVCs. This includes average technology intensity at various stages of the GVC.

Table A1 Full list of indicators in the database, by file

A. File *DB_Structural_Change_Basic_Indicators.xlsx*

Data on sectoral structure:

Value-added share	Sectoral share in total value of the economy
Household consumption share	Sectoral share in total household consumption of the economy
Total demand share	Sectoral share in total demand of the economy

Data on change of sectoral structure:

NAV for value added	Norm of Absolute Values (NAV), Structural change indicator for value added
NAV for household consumption	Norm of Absolute Values (NAV), Structural change indicator for household consumption
NAV for total demand	Norm of Absolute Values (NAV), Structural change indicator for total demand

Data on GVC structure of trade (set of 29 indicators, each for exports and imports):

ExportsTotal or ImportsTotal	Total value of exports or imports
CapitalShare	Share of capital goods in total exports or imports
ConsumerShare	Share of consumer goods in total exports or imports
IntermediateShare	Share of intermediate goods in total exports or imports
CapitalRCA	Value of Revealed Comparative Advantage (RCA) indicator for capital goods in total exports or imports
ConsumerRCA	Value of Revealed Comparative Advantage (RCA) indicator for consumer goods in total exports or imports
IntermediateRCA	Value of Revealed Comparative Advantage (RCA) indicator for intermediate goods in total exports or imports
Intermediate_Generic_sh	Share of generic intermediates in total exports or imports
Intermediate_Specific_sh	Share of specific intermediates in total exports or imports
Intermediate_Mixed_sh	Share of mixed (generic/specific) intermediates in total exports or imports
Intermediate_NC_sh	Share of non-classified intermediates in total exports or imports
Capital_Generic_sh	Share of generic capital goods in total exports or imports
Capital_Specific_sh	Share of specific capital goods in total exports or imports
Capital_Mixed_sh	Share of mixed (generic/specific) capital goods in total exports or imports
Intermediate_GenericRCA	Value of Revealed Comparative Advantage (RCA) indicator for generic intermediates in total exports or imports

(*Continued*)

10 *Innovation and Structural Transformation in Asia*

Table A1 (Continued)

Intermediate_SpecificRCA	Value of Revealed Comparative Advantage (RCA) indicator for specific intermediates in total exports or imports
Intermediate_MixedRCA	Value of Revealed Comparative Advantage (RCA) indicator for mixed intermediates in total exports or imports
Intermediate_NCRCA	Value of Revealed Comparative Advantage (RCA) indicator for non-classified intermediates in total exports or imports
Capital_GenericRCA	Value of Revealed Comparative Advantage (RCA) indicator for generic capital goods in total exports or imports
Capital_SpecificRCA	Value of Revealed Comparative Advantage (RCA) indicator for specific capital goods in total exports or imports
Capital_MixedRCA	Value of Revealed Comparative Advantage (RCA) indicator for mixed capital goods in total exports or imports
Consumer_Primary_sh	Share of primary consumer goods in total exports or imports
Consumer_Processed_sh	Share of processed consumer goods in total exports or imports
Intermediate_Primary_sh	Share of primary intermediates in total exports or imports
Intermediate_Processed_sh	Share of processed intermediates in total exports or imports
Consumer_PrimaryRCA	Value of Revealed Comparative Advantage (RCA) indicator for primary consumer goods in total exports or imports
Consumer_ProcessedRCA	Value of Revealed Comparative Advantage (RCA) indicator for processed consumer goods in total exports or imports
Intermediate_PrimaryRCA	Value of Revealed Comparative Advantage (RCA) indicator for primary intermediates in total exports or imports
Intermediate_ProcessedRCA	Value of Revealed Comparative Advantage (RCA) indicator for processed intermediates in total exports or imports

Data on trade in Fourth Industrial Revolution products (set of 36 indicators, each for exports and imports):

CADCAM exports or imports	Value of exports or imports of CADCAM technologies
ICT exports or imports	Value of exports or imports of ICT technologies
RegInstr exports or imports	Value of exports or imports of Regulating Instruments technologies
Robots exports or imports	Value of exports or imports of Robot technologies
Welding exports or imports	value of exports or imports of Welding technologies
3D exports or imports	Value of exports or imports of 3D printing technologies
Non-4IR exports or imports	Value of exports or imports of all other products (i.e., non-4IR products)

(Continued)

Table A1 (Continued)

4IR exports or imports	Value of 4IR exports or imports (i.e., the sum of the different 4IR categories)
Total exports or imports	Value of total exports or imports
CADCAM_sh	Share of CADCAM technologies in total exports or imports
ICT_sh	Share of ICT technologies in total exports or imports
RegInstr_sh	Share of Regulating Instruments technologies in total exports or imports
Robots_sh	Share of Robot technologies in total exports or imports
Welding_sh	Share of Welding technologies in total exports or imports
3D_sh	Share of 3D printing technologies in total exports or imports
4IR_sh	Share of all 4IR products in total exports or imports
Other_sh	Share of all other products in total exports or imports
RCA_CADCAM	Value of Revealed Comparative Advantage (RCA) indicator in the export of CADCAM technologies
RCA_ICT	Value of Revealed Comparative Advantage (RCA) indicator in the export of ICT technologies
RCA_RegInstr	Value of Revealed Comparative Advantage (RCA) indicator in the export of Regulating Instruments technologies
RCA_Robots	Value of Revealed Comparative Advantage (RCA) indicator in the export of Robot technologies
RCA_Welding	Value of Revealed Comparative Advantage (RCA) indicator in the export of Welding technologies
RCA_3D	Value of Revealed Comparative Advantage (RCA) indicator in the export of 3D printing technologies
RCA_4IR	Value of Revealed Comparative Advantage (RCA) indicator in the export of aggregate 4IR technologies
CADCAM_4IRsh	Share of CADCAM technologies in 4IR exports or imports
ICT_4IRsh	Share of ICT technologies in 4IR exports or imports
RegInstr_4IRsh	Share of Regulating Instruments technologies in 4IR exports or imports
Robots_4IRsh	Share of Robot technologies in 4IR exports or imports
Welding_4IRsh	Share of Welding technologies in 4IR exports or imports
3D_4IRsh	Share of 3D printing technologies in 4IR exports or imports
RCA_4IR_CADCAM	Value of Revealed Comparative Advantage (RCA) indicator in the export of CADCAM technologies with 4IR exports or imports
RCA_4IR_ICT	Value of Revealed Comparative Advantage (RCA) indicator in the export of ICT technologies with 4IR exports or imports
RCA_4IR_RegInstr	Value of Revealed Comparative Advantage (RCA) indicator in the export of Regulating Instruments technologies with 4IR exports or imports

(*Continued*)

Table A1 (Continued)

RCA_4IR_Robots	Value of Revealed Comparative Advantage (RCA) indicator in the export of Robot technologies with 4IR exports or imports
RCA_4IR_Welding	Value of Revealed Comparative Advantage (RCA) indicator in the export of Welding technologies with 4IR exports or imports
RCA_4IR_3D	Value of Revealed Comparative Advantage (RCA) indicator in the export of 3D printing technologies with 4IR exports or imports

B. File *DB_Structural_Change_ProductivityGrowth.xlsx*

Data on employment and value added growth, by sector:

Employment index	Index of employment per sector (2015 = 100)
VA index	Index of value added in 2015 prices per sector (2015 = 100)

Data on productivity and shares, by sector:

Labor productivity index	Index of labor productivity per sector (2015 = 100)
Labor productivity in thousands of 2005 US$ per worker	Labor productivity in thousands of 2015 US$ per worker (for total economy)
Real exchange rate factor	Real exchange rate factor (= GDP in 2015 PPP$/ GDP in 2015 US$)
Relative sectoral productivity	Relative sectoral labor productivity (sector productivity/total economy productivity)
Employment share	Share of employment of the sector in the total economy
Value-added share	Share of value added of the sector in the total economy

Data on productivity decompositions:

Productivity growth	Average annual labor productivity growth, for various periods
WS	The within-sector effect as it contributes to labor productivity growth, for various periods
SSRE	The static structural change effect as it contributes to labor productivity growth, for various periods
DSRE	The dynamic structural change effect as it contributes to labor productivity growth, for various periods

Data on structural change:

NAVSC	The Norm of Absolute Values (NAV) indicator for structural change, for various periods

Data on building blocks for productivity decompositions:

Changes of shares	The change of the employment share, for various periods
Relative productivity	Relative (to the total economy) sectoral labor productivity level at the start of the period, for various periods

(*Continued*)

Table A1 (Continued)

Change of productivity	The change of sectoral labor productivity relative to sectoral labor productivity of the total economy at the beginning of the period, for various periods
Share	The share of employment at the beginning of the period, for various periods

C. File *DB_Input_And_Output_Complexities.xlsx*

Total input complexity	Input complexity of all domestic and foreign value (total) into the chain
Domestic input complexity	Input complexity of domestic value into the chain
Foreign input complexity	Input complexity of foreign value into the chain
Output complexity	Output complexity of the chain (final goods)
Intermediate goods complexity	Complexity of intermediate goods of the sector (output)
Overall complexity	Complexity of all goods (final and intermediate) of the sector (output)

D. File *DB_Upgrading_Capabilities.xlsx*

Indicators for existing specialization profile:

Diversification	Diversification index of the country-sector combination
Standardness	Standardness index of the country-sector combination
Potential	Potential complexity gain index of the country-sector combination
Fitness	Average complexity of the country-sector combination

Indicators for upgrading potential:

Short run upgrade probability bonus	Measure for relatedness, short run
Short run potential complexity gain	Measure for complexity gain, short run
Short run share of products with RCA	Measure for existing specialization profile
Long run upgrade probability bonus	Measure for relatedness, long run
Long run potential complexity gain	Measure for complexity gain, long run
Long run share of products with RCA	Measure for existing specialization profile, long-run potential

E. File *DB_IR4patents_2000_2019.xlsx*

Patent indicators for Fourth Industrial Revolution technologies:

Nr Families	Number of patent families per IR4 subfield
Nr Families 10 year Cumulative	Number of patent families per IR4 subfield, 10-year cumulative (up to and including indicated year)
Share Subfield in Total IR4	Share of IR4 subfield in total IR4 patent families

(*Continued*)

Table A1 (Continued)

Share Subfield in Total IR4 10-year Cumulative	Share of IR4 subfield in total IR4 patent families, 10-year cumulative (up to and including indicated year)
Share IR4 Subfield in All Technologies	Share of IR4 subfield in patent families of all technologies
Share IR4 Subfield in All Technologies 10-year Cumulative	Share of IR4 subfield in patent families of all technologies, 10-year cumulative (up to and including indicated year)

Patent indicators for all technologies:

Nr Families All Technologies	Number of patent families all technologies
Nr Families All Technologies 10-year Cumulative	Number of patent families all technologies, 10-year cumulative (up to and including indicated year)

F. File *DB_Patents_Embedded_in_GVCs.xlsx*

Indicators about patenting intensity of GVCs:

Patent intensity in own value added	Patents per unit of own value added, all fields and 4IR fields
Patent intensity in all value added used	Patents per unit of value added used, all fields and 4IR fields
Patent intensity in contributions by foreign value chains	Patents per unit of value added used supplied by foreign sectors, all fields and 4IR fields
Patent intensity in contributions by domestic value chains	Patents per unit of value added used supplied by other domestic sectors, all fields and 4IR fields
Patent intensity in domestically purchased products (all technology fields)	Patents per unit of final demand, all fields and 4IR fields

G. File *DB_GVC_Integration.xlsx*

Basic indicators on GVC integration:

Backward linkages, foreign share	Foreign share of total demand served
Backward linkages, other domestic sectors share	Other domestic sectors share of total demand served
Backward linkages, own sector share	Own sector share of total demand served
Domestic Backward VC Integration	Domestic Backward Value Chain Integration (other domestic as a share of other domestic plus foreign)
Forward linkages, foreign share	Foreign share of total value added produced
Forward linkages, other domestic sectors share	Other domestic sectors share of total value added produced
Forward linkages, own sector share	Own sector share of total value added produced
Domestic Forward VC Integration	Domestic Forward Value Chain Integration (other domestic as a share of other domestic plus foreign)

(*Continued*)

Table A1 (Continued)

Value and Balassa index data on GVC integration:

Total Final Demand	Value-Added Exports of Economy to Global Sectors (Balassa Index and USD values)
Value-Added Exports of Economy to Global Sectors (USD Values)	Value-Added Exports of Economy-Sector to Global Economies (Balassa Index and USD values)
Value-Added Exports of Economy-Sector To Global Economies (USD Values)	Intermediate Product Exports (Gross) of Economy to Global Sectors (Balassa Index and USD values)
Intermediate Product Exports (Gross) of Economy to Global Sectors (USD Values)	Intermediate Product Exports (Gross) of Economy-Sector to Global Economies (Balassa Index and USD values)
Intermediate Product Exports (Gross) of Economy-Sector to Global Economies (USD Values)	Final Product Exports of Economy-Sector to Global Economies (Balassa Index and USD values)
Final Product Exports of Economy-Sector to Global Economies (USD Values)	All Product Exports (Gross) of Economy-Sector to Global Economies (Balassa Index and USD values)
All Product Exports (Gross) of Economy-Sector to Global Economies (USD Values)	Value-Added Imports of Economy from Global Sectors (Balassa Index and USD values)
Value-Added Imports of Economy from Global Sectors (USD Values)	Value-Added Imports of Economy-Sector from Global Economies (Balassa Index and USD values)
Value-Added Imports of Economy-Sector from Global Economies (USD Values)	Intermediate Product Imports (Gross) of Economy from Global Sectors (Balassa Index and USD values)
Intermediate Product Imports (Gross) of Economy from Global Sectors (USD Values)	Intermediate Product Imports (Gross) of Economy-Sector from Global Economies (Balassa Index and USD values)
Intermediate Product Imports (Gross) of Economy-Sector from Global Economies (USD Values)	Final Product Imports of Economy from Global Sectors (Balassa Index and USD values)
Final Product Imports of Economy From Global Sectors (USD Values)	All Product Imports (Gross) of Economy from Global Sectors (Balassa Index and USD values)
All Product Imports (Gross) of Economy from Global Sectors (USD Values)	Total final demand (only for total economy/all sectors)

H. File *DB_GVC_Radius.xlsx*

Data on regionalization of GVCs:

Backward geo-radius	Average standardized distance for backward integration
Forward geo-radius	Average standardized distance for forward integration

Note

1 https://www.adb.org/what-we-do/data/regional-input-output-tables.

2 Introduction to Asia's Development

2.1 Introduction: Different Views About Asia's Development

By the mid-1990s, it became obvious that Hong Kong, Japan, Singapore, South Korea, and Taiwan had attained phenomenal growth rates, 7%–10% per annum since the mid-1960s. They were all high-income economies. A large literature emerged trying to explain these economies' phenomenal performance. This was a very important question for development because it appeared that what these economies had done defied the neoclassical orthodoxy: governments intervened, and factor prices were distorted to allocate resources to certain sectors.

Explaining these economies' fast growth was key. One strand of the literature followed the neoclassical decomposition of output growth into the contributions of labor and capital and that of total factor productivity growth. This way, Young (1992, 1994, 1995), for example, argued that their growth had been mostly the result of factor accumulation. The contribution of total factor productivity had been much smaller.

Another strand of the literature understood the region's growth from a different angle. Amsden (1989) and Wade (1990), among others, argued that firms in these economies accumulated capabilities very fast and that the role of the government was fundamental to understand their progress. Under this view, the East Asian governments undertook major responsibility for the promotion of economic growth through a series of financial and non-financial measures. However, it is difficult to ascertain which specific policies contributed to the success of these economies, and also to guess what would have happened in the absence of such policies.

The tension between the two strands of the literature was clear in the World Bank's (1993) analysis of East Asia's miracle and in the comments by Amsden (1994), Kwon (1994), and Stiglitz (1996). Felipe and McCombie (2003) offered a methodological critique of the neoclassical growth accounting approach.

Whatever these five economies did, the fact is that they attained high income during the 1990s (Japan had attained it earlier). Certainly, Japan was part of the Asian miracle, but its phenomenal performance had started decades earlier. China also joined this group as it was documented that it had achieved very high growth rates of GDP since the 1980s. A few other Asian countries have also done well (e.g., Indonesia, Malaysia, Thailand), but their record does not match that of the other six economies. Other Asian countries such as Vietnam have come to the scene much more recently, and only time will tell us how far they manage to go. Large economies in terms of population like India, Pakistan, Bangladesh, and the Philippines have had periods of acceptable performance, but these were not sustained and they lag far behind.

The view implicit in this book is closer to the second one, the one that explained East Asia's growth and progress through the increase in firms' capabilities and the role of the government. Further, we argue that it is not possible to comprehend Asia's development (not only that of the most successful economies) without bringing into the discussion the significant structural transformation that these economies underwent since the mid-1960s, both from the point of view of output and employment. The shift of workers out of agriculture into industry and services happened because these economies created companies with capabilities to manufacture products of increasing complexity. These capabilities allowed these economies to upgrade their export structures. The role of the government facilitating and encouraging structural transformation through different tools of industrial policy was crucial.

We also argue that these economies grew fast and for a long time because they did not run into balance of payments problems, as argued by the balance-of-payments-constrained-growth model, which relates structural upgrading (shifting into exports with a higher income elasticity of demand) and market expansion, to the relaxation of the balance of payments constraint (Thirlwall 1979). The successful East Asian economies started their development after WWII by following different versions of import substitution. This was a consequence of the economic situation after independence, especially the acute shortage of foreign exchange. In the case of South Korea, for example, the priority industries before the 1960s were sugar, fertilizer, spun yarn, cement, and glass. This was also the case with Taiwan, which, to support its import-substitution policy, controlled foreign exchange, erected protective tariffs, imposed import restrictions, and had multiple exchange rates. Under these conditions, there was a conscious effort to replace imports of non-durable consumer goods with domestic production. This way, the production of synthetic yarn, bicycles, flour, plastic, artificial fibers, glass, cement, fertilizers, apparel, wood, leather, and cotton textiles increased significantly. Even Singapore toyed with import substitution before 1965. After independence, the government concluded that the shift in industrialization that the country needed could only be induced by implementing an export-led program. Officials realized that a small economy like Singapore had to think in terms of selling to the markets of the industrialized economies.

In what follows, we review the literature on structural transformation and capability upgrading. In this context, we bring into the discussion the role of GVCs and the possible impact of digital technologies. We also discuss the role of industrial policy, and the balance-of-payment constrained growth rate.

2.2 Structural Transformation and the Accumulation of Capabilities

The economic transformation of the successful East Asian economies is best summarized in the transfer of workers out of agriculture (the sector with the lowest productivity) into industry (manufacturing growth) (Kaldor 1967), and second, in the diversification and upgrading of their export baskets. As documented by Felipe et al. (2016), the share of agricultural employment in total employment in South Korea and Taiwan declined much faster during their period of high growth, at about 1 percentage point per annum, than it had done in the Western advanced economies in the 19th and the earlier part of the 20th centuries. This is the essence of development: the movement of workers out of low-productivity activities into high-productivity activities, in particular into manufacturing. The decompositions of productivity growth into the "within sectors" and "structural transformation" (the shift of workers from sectors of lower into sectors of higher productivity) components undertaken by the Asian Development Bank (2013) and Rodrik et al. (2017) are very helpful to understand the sources of growth. They indicate that both components (within-sectors productivity growth and structural transformation) were significant in these economies. Szirmai (2012) documented that all historical examples of success in economic development and catch-up since 1870 have been associated with successful industrialization. The Asian Development Bank (2013) provided a thorough analysis of Asia's economic transformation and highlighted the significant differences across economies. Industrialization played a key role in East Asia's development in the 20th century but not in most other Asian countries. Szirmai and Verspagen (2015) also highlighted the importance of manufacturing for development and documented interaction effects of manufacturing with education and income gaps. Related to this, Felipe et al. (2019) showed that attaining a minimum share of manufacturing employment in total employment (18%–20%) for some time was much more important than attaining a high manufacturing output share, in order to attain high income per capita.

Szirmai and Verspagen (2015) concluded that since 1990, manufacturing has become a more difficult route to growth than before. This last finding was corroborated by Felipe et al. (2019), in the context of the recent discussions about deindustrialization. While this is a phenomenon well documented in the advanced economies, the recent literature has shown that it is affecting many developing countries but at lower levels of income per capita, hence the reference to premature deindustrialization. Indeed, while developed countries could ride the manufacturing escalator up to relatively high levels of per capita income, and the manufacturing employment share attained was very high (about 30%), today's developing countries reach a much lower manufacturing peak (15%) and at a lower income per capita. Felipe and Mehta (2016) argue that the world has not deindustrialized as documented by the fact that the worldwide output and employment shares have remained constant. What varied was the country composition, with the biggest winner being China.

Apart from the changes in the employment structure, another key contributing factor to East Asian growth was the change in the product mix. The recent literature on the product space of Hidalgo et al. (2007) and the concept of complexity of Hidalgo and Hausmann (2009) make the very important point that not all products have the same consequences for development. This work explains economic development as a process of learning how to produce (and export) more complex products. Using network theory methods, they have shown that the development path of a country is strongly influenced by its existing product mix: some pairs of products are more closely related to each other than others, and it is easier to learn to make products related to those that a country already produces. In addition, countries with an initial comparative advantage in complex products are able to branch out into more products. Branching out, or achieving dynamic competitive advantage, is a core goal of development, partly because the production of more complex products is associated with higher national incomes and wages, and also because countries that establish a presence in a new export industry tend to then converge toward global productivity levels in that industry (Hausmann et al. 2007). This literature, in effect, implies that development is slow for countries with productive structures geared toward low-productivity and low-wage activities, producing mostly low-valued commodities or agricultural products. Development is fast, on the other hand, for countries with productive structures geared toward high-productivity and high-wage activities.

While the East Asian economies' export mixes in 1962 were somewhat more diverse and complex than those of other countries in the region (e.g., the Philippines and Indonesia provide a contrasting comparison), their dynamism was far greater. Hong Kong, Singapore, South Korea, and Taiwan developed comparative advantages in many more products and in more complex products over the course of the next three decades, and grew rapidly as they did so (Felipe et al. 2012 Hausmann et al. 2014).

The product space and the complexity literatures have interpreted the fact that diversity and complexity predict growth in causal terms. The presumed mechanism is the development of "capabilities" (Hidalgo and Hausmann 2009).[1] These could be (a) the set of human and physical capital, the legal system, and institutions, among others, that are needed to produce a product (hence, they are product-specific, not just a set of amorphous factor inputs); (b) at the firm level, the "know-how" and working practices held collectively by the group of individuals comprising the firm; and (c) the organizational abilities that provide the capacity to form, manage, and operate activities that involve large numbers of people. The last two are referred to as technical and organizational capabilities. According to Sutton (2001, 2005), capabilities manifest themselves in quality-productivity combinations. A given capability is embodied in the tacit knowledge of the individuals who comprise the firm's workforce. The quality-productivity combinations are not a continuum from zero; rather, there is a window with a "minimum threshold" below which the firm would be excluded from the market, and not export (see also Kremer 1993; Melitz 2003). Therefore, capabilities are largely non-tradable inputs. Khan (2015) argues that because they reflect mostly tacit knowledge, the way to acquire them is through learning-by-doing (LBD). Such LBD requires external (to the firm) financing, i.e., it has to be subsidized. Simultaneously, it requires efforts on the part of both the firm and worker.

Through this lens, economic development is a process that requires acquiring more complex sets of capabilities to move toward new activities associated with higher levels of productivity. In the case of the East Asian economies, the implication is that their success in industrial upgrading ignited processes of capability improvement, including some measure of technology development, human capital accumulation, and institutional development.

The literatures on structural transformation and the product space empirically link growth in the East Asian economies to success in changing what they produced (toward more complex manufactures) and highlight the cumulative, path-dependent nature of these changes. However, they are agnostic about which capabilities matter and provide no specific explanation of *how and why* these changes came about (Lee 2024). This matters because almost every other developing economy has attempted to alter its production mix, but few have succeeded. The two key barriers have been how to ensure that firms introducing products and technologies that are new to the country thrive; and maintaining stability on the balance of payments during the industrialization process.

Schumpeterian work on technological development has helped dispel the naïve view that simple price advantages – undervalued currencies and wage advantages – and the ability to imitate widely used technologies could explain success in industrialization. It emphasizes that the adoption of new production technologies happens under specific conditions ("windows of opportunity") and that economies whose firms are able to adopt less mature technologies are more likely to undergo techno-economic paradigm shifts (including institutional changes) that produce durable economic leads. Success in young technologies is therefore difficult and rare, but valuable (Saviotti and Pyka 2011; Malerba and Lee 2021; Lee 2024).

Perez and Soete (1988) provide a classic description of the circumstances under which firms and countries are able to adopt new production technologies and produce new products.[2] They emphasize that success requires overcoming multiple thresholds, each being a function of the technology and its maturity, and that firms and the countries that host them are differentiated in their capacities to overcome these constraints. Specifically, they argue that as technologies mature, adopting them comes to require less scientific knowledge and fewer locational advantages – and therefore less government support. However, adopting a mature production technology requires more investment than adopting a young technology, and the amount of tacit knowledge and experience required to adopt a technology increases and then decreases over its life cycle.

As a consequence, the most mature technologies, like those involved in garments, footwear, and assembly manufacturing, are easy to adopt, provided that adequate investment capital can be secured, but offer less opportunities for learning and fierce competition. Mid-maturity technologies like cars, steel, and petrochemicals, between the 1960s and 1990s, are the most difficult to adopt, requiring extraordinary amounts of tacit knowledge and heavy investment. Younger technologies, like, at the time, those involved in making electronics, were possible to adopt in countries with access to an adequate scientific workforce and governments capable of creating locational advantages, even if they lacked capital. Moreover, early adopters of these young technologies were often able to build durable knowledge leads, cemented by increases in R&D and institutional changes manifested in national innovation systems and education expansions (Freeman 1988). These, in turn, spur entry into new sectors – a process that matches the empirical patterns picked up in the complexity literature (Saviotti and Pyka 2011).

This body of Schumpeterian theory helps explain the East Asian economies' success in the 1960s, 1970s, and 1980s.[3] Capable firms with great capacity to assimilate foreign technologies and ultimately to develop their own were key. The East Asian economies had business-friendly, pragmatic governments (and some had FDI-friendly policies), willing to deploy industrial policies to reduce locational disadvantages in order to facilitate technological change. Singapore also benefited from its position on the Malacca Strait, while South Korea and Taiwan's close ties to the United States facilitated investment (Studwell 2013).

Under these circumstances, it is not surprising that electronics – the key young technology between the 1960s and 1990s – featured prominently in the export mixes of Hong Kong, Singapore, South Korea, and Taiwan, by 1990. In Singapore, Taiwan, and South Korea, this early success in electronics, built through collaboration with Western multinational firms, has manifestly translated into durable technological leads. The East Asian economies also made some inroads by the 1990s into technologies of middle maturity – South Korea into cars, and all of them in products manufactured from petrochemicals like plastic products and synthetic rubber, fiber, and fabric; industries linked backward to chemicals and metallurgical products, which were produced in modest amounts by all four in the 1960s.[4]

A significant part of this progress took place in the context of GVCs (Hobday 1995a). The significance of GVCs has become more obvious recently as these have expanded and their importance for trade has increased. GVCs are now seen as a vehicle for economic development (though this is controversial), allowing economies to integrate into the global economy and to industrialize by specializing in certain activities within a product's value chain. Although there is significant heterogeneity, the evidence suggests that overall GVC integration of the Asian countries increased over time.

Having said this, the upgrading process was not easy. Hobday (1995a) described in detail how East Asian firms from Hong Kong, South Korea, Singapore, and Taiwan climbed the ladder by slowly learning by doing. In the specific case of the electronics industry, he concluded that the East Asian latecomers engaged in a painstaking and cumulative process of technological learning (Hobday 1995b, 1188). Kim (1997, 129) described Hyundai's efforts to produce a car after it had purchased foreign equipment, hired expatriate consultants, and signed licensing agreements with foreign firms. Despite the training and consulting services of experts, Hyundai engineers repeated trials and errors for 14 months before creating the first prototype. They had to implement 2,888 engine design changes.

The actions taken by the East Asian firms and governments to produce these successes in nascent and mid-stage technologies are noteworthy. They include firm-level efforts to imitate and innovate and governments industrial policies. Dosi et al. (2020) explain why these activities by firms and governments are complementary.

Finally, and in the context of the analysis of structural transformation and capability building, we also add the expectations created in recent years by the 4IR technologies. These technologies include robotics, additive manufacturing, artificial intelligence, the internet of things, and big data. These have raised expectations about significant changes in the way we live, work, and interact. This has to do with the potential that the new technologies have to create General-Purpose Technologies that truly change life. These are technologies being developed mostly by the advanced economies. What is the role of the Asian economies in the generation of 4IR technologies?

2.3 The Role of Industrial Policy

Arguably, this is the most contested ingredient of East Asia's success, and it is difficult to present an unbiased account of this topic. Young's (1992) thesis about Singapore was that its lack of total factor productivity growth had been caused by its industrial policies. This view was heavily contested at the time. The World Bank (1993) itself ended up containing a mix of somewhat contradictory statements on the role of industrial policy. Pack and Saggi (2006) reviewed the empirical evidence in support of the use of industrial policy for correcting market failures that plague the process of industrialization. They concluded that public interventions played a limited role.[5] On the other side of the story, Wade (1990) and Jomo and Wah (1999) provide detailed accounts of the instruments used and the positive role of industrial policy in East Asia.

Although historically many cases of industrial policy failed, we also believe that achieving growth rates that approached 10% per annum for long periods required more than deciding to export and to get into manufactures. Authors like Amsden (1989), Wade (1990), and Cimoli et al. (2009) have argued that this additional ingredient was active governments that directed and consciously accelerated industrial development by implementing policies that defied comparative advantage based on static allocative efficiency, which leads developing countries to specialize in labor-intensive products. Static allocative efficiency is silent on the question of what countries should do as labor becomes scarce and expensive, which forces them to enter capital-intensive sectors. Instead, the East Asian governments promoted dynamic efficiency. This is based on the idea that firms (and ultimately a country) adapt and improve productivity over time in response to changing markets, technologies, and customer preferences. Dynamic efficiency involves continuous improvement, investment in new technologies, and a focus on long-term growth. Stiglitz (1996) also argued that East Asian governments undertook major responsibility for the promotion of economic growth. He admitted that it is difficult to ascertain which specific policies contributed to the success of these economies (the attribution problem), and also to guess what would have happened in the absence of such policies. Moreover, that the government subsidized a sector that grew rapidly does not imply that the growth should be attributed to the government's action. Because the ingredients that led to success were interactive (i.e., contrary to what growth accounting does), and because they were introduced in conjunction with other policies, the role of government has to be evaluated in the context of a package.

The intellectual underpinnings of government intervention in Asia go back to Gerschenkron's (1962) *latecomer model*, the idea of which is that, without the government pushing to alter the structure of production of the economy toward advanced industries (from light manufacturing and agriculture into ships, steel, autos, industrial machinery, and electronics), growth and development would have happened much more slowly in these poor (latecomer) countries. What this means is that the ultimate purpose of industrial policy and targeting certain sectors was more than addressing market failures but to induce distortions in the short term in order to realize gains in the long term. Two decades later, Johnson (1982) referred to these states as *developmental states*.

Amsden (1989, 1995) used this model to explain East Asia's success. The experience of East Asia's latecomers shows that they focused on industries that had dominant technologies. These are industries where competition is based on cost minimization and on the building of mass production capacities as fast as possible. The experience of Asia's late industrializers (starting with

Japan after WWII) also shows that they all had effective developmental states that provided extensive support to their firms, not only by boosting the profits of those firms that were prepared to enter the competitive arena, through subsidies, tax breaks, or low interest rates loans but also through mechanisms designed to curb rent-seeking. Some of the most cited cases are those of South Korea and Taiwan, where governments provided support in terms of subsidies or tax breaks *in exchange* (i.e., reciprocity) for firms achieving certain export targets. Failure to meet these targets would lead to withdrawal of the support. This was very much a results-oriented performance mechanism. It proved to be a powerful means to discipline both governments and firms, and to control rent-seeking. All this assistance to their firms was complemented by a complex set of catch-up institutions, such as the Singapore Economic Development Board, or Taiwan's Industrial Technology Research Institute, whose goal was to capture technologies and raise the skills levels. The industrialization problem, namely, whether development of a modern capitalist industry can be possible in a backward country (e.g., Cambodia, Lao PDR, Bangladesh, India), is as relevant today as it was in the 1960s and 1970s.

Comparing the old advanced economies (including Japan) with Hong Kong, South Korea, Singapore, Taiwan, as well as with Indonesia, Malaysia, and Thailand, Amsden (1995) elaborated upon the latecomer industrialization model and highlighted three important differences. First, on the question of why latecomers needed more government, she claimed that "industrial policy was invented to raise productivity levels" (Amsden 1995, 792), given that the two other options to lower unit labor costs were to lower nominal wages, or to miss industrialization at all.

Second, Amsden argued that the actual experience about the degree of government intervention in the economy did not squarely follow Gerschenkron's prediction that there would be more intervention the more backward the country. Rather, intervention was greater in countries with smaller *competitive assets* in relation to global competitive needs. A competitive asset is anything that contributes to the international competitiveness of raw labor power and raises labor productivity, e.g., being a port, being endowed with natural resources. Why did the British government not intervene heavily in Hong Kong – with the exception of providing mass subsidized housing, which lowered labor costs? Because in the 1950s and 1960s, the colony was able to access the Commonwealth preferences, which provided it with a market shielded from Japanese competition in clothing and textiles. Hong Kong also had a significant inflow of experienced textile engineers and technicians who had moved after the Chinese revolution. Indonesia, Malaysia, and Thailand also had a competitive asset, a natural resource base; hence, government intervention was modest initially. It increased as time passed by as these countries sought to diversify their economies because all three lacked a key competitive asset, namely, entrepreneurial skills. Government intervened in Japan, but it was the first Asian country to undergo a full industrial revolution starting in the 19th century, and it had developed an industrial base before WWII. The governments that intervened the most were those of South Korea, Singapore, and Taiwan. The reason was that they lacked competitive assets. Although Singapore was a port, at the time of independence in 1965 its economy, with two million people and land area of only 581 km^2, was adrift. The other two were in political disarray in the 1950s.

Third, Amsden argued that the governments of Japan and Hong Kong, Singapore, South Korea, and Taiwan did a better job than those of Indonesia, Malaysia, and Thailand because they were much more forceful applying the reciprocity principle of providing subsidies in exchange for performance standards, often in the form of export targets. This system of reciprocity disciplined both firms and the government itself. Interventions in the first group were of higher quality because their bureaucracies were of higher quality.

Finally, recent years have witnessed a revival of the work on industrial policy. Using input-output data, Lane (2022) provides novel evidence of the positive role of industrial policies in South Korea. Juhász et al. (2023) survey the recent literature on the subject and conclude that it offers a more positive take on industrial policy. They argue that industrial policy is being reshaped by a new understanding of governance, a richer set of policy instruments beyond subsidies, and the reality of deindustrialization.

2.4 The Balance-of-Payments-Constrained Growth Rate Model

We add to the discussion of structural transformation *cum* upgrading and industrial policy, the insights provided by the balance-of-payments-constrained (BOPC) growth rate model of Thirlwall (1979). This is a demand-driven model in which the key growth constraint is the need to maintain a dynamic equilibrium in the current account because most developing countries cannot permanently finance current account deficits, not the availability of factors of production. The simplest version of this model is that the BOPC growth (y_B) rate is $y_B = \left(\frac{\varepsilon}{\pi}\right)z$, where ε and π are, respectively, the income elasticities of demand of exports and imports and z is the growth rate of the country's trading partners. This expression means that to attain a faster actual growth rate without facing current account problems, a developing country has to increase its balance-of-payments-constrained growth rate y_B. This rate will increase as a result of a higher growth rate by its trading partners (z), and/or a higher $\left(\frac{\varepsilon}{\pi}\right)$. These two elasticities are summaries of the non-price characteristics of exports and imports (quality, variety, reliability, speed of delivery, or distribution network). As a country imports products with a higher income elasticity, it will have to export products with a higher income elasticity.

Under this view, the East Asian economies exported to economies that were expanding and growing fast, and transformed their export structures, and this showed up in a higher $\left(\frac{\varepsilon}{\pi}\right)$. This result and idea are consistent with the notion of an increasing complexity as explained above. This higher ratio allowed these economies to grow faster and, at the same time, relax the balance-of-payments constraint. Felipe et al. (2019) and Felipe and Lanzafame (2020) provide estimates of the balance-of-payments-constrained growth rate for Indonesia and China, respectively.

Notes

1 There is now a well-established literature on the importance of capabilities in various contexts, and from different schools. For example, Acemoglu and Zillibotti (1999) advanced a theoretical explanation for the wide variation in the stock of knowledge across countries. They argued that societies accumulate knowledge by repeating certain tasks and that scarcity of capital restricts the repetition of various activities. Kremer (1993) referred to the crucial role of capabilities in the context of development, and Lall (1992) and Bell and Pavitt (1995) analyzed the role of capabilities from an innovation and development point of view.
2 Later contributors to this literature emphasize late-stage developments in latecomer economies, including R&D expansions and role reversals wherein their firms in latecomer economies become technology leaders (Malerba and Lee 2021; Lee 2024). Here, we work with the classic literature that focuses more on earlier phases of capability development more typical of the East Asian economies prior to the 1990s.
3 Ang and Madsen (2011) tested the power of two second-generation endogenous neoclassical growth models, to explain the growth of the East Asian miracle economies. They conclude that the Schumpeterian model, where innovative activity and R&D play a fundamental role, can explain these economies' growth. These models are still based on the neoclassical growth model. See Felipe et al. (2025) on this.
4 Certainly, industries already operating with mature technologies at the time, like garments, footwear, luggage, and toys, became very important in Hong Kong, South Korea, and Taiwan, where labor was not a constraint, but this was also true in less successful Southeast Asian economies, as predicted by theories of technology life cycles.
5 We note two points on the critical evaluation of industrial policy by Pack and Saggi (2006). First, they cite authors who studied the impact of industrial policy on total factor productivity growth (see Felipe et al. 2025 on this). Second, they highlight experiences like that of India, perhaps not the most enlightening.

3 Labor Productivity and Structural Transformation in Asia

3.1 Introduction: Labor Productivity Is Key to Improving Standards of Living

Labor productivity, the ratio of output to employment, is key to increasing income per capita. What factors affect labor productivity? Since labor productivity is intrinsically a firm-level concept, one could analyze the internal factors that determine it. These are the factors that operate within the firm and are under the control of management, e.g., mechanization, workforce skills, product quality, and organizational capabilities. Likewise, one could talk about the external factors that affect labor productivity. These are the factors that operate indirectly through the environment by affecting producers' willingness and ability to harness factors that affect firms, e.g., competition, infrastructure, or the overall level of formal education.

At the aggregate level, labor productivity matters because it is the key component of output per person. Indeed, this can be written as the product of the ratio of employment to population times labor productivity. As noted above, this last variable is of great importance in most economies and is key in order to understand economies' long-run performance.

Growth in aggregate labor productivity is, in turn, determined by developments at the sectoral level. In particular, aggregate labor productivity growth will occur if there is labor productivity growth within the sectors of the economy, or if the structure of production shifts toward sectors that themselves have higher labor productivity. In other words, aggregate labor productivity growth is driven by developments in productivity within sectors (which can be driven by technical progress, for example) and by structural change (i.e., employment shifts across sectors). In recent years, the role of structural change as a driver of aggregate economic performance has re-emerged in academic and policy debates (Foster-McGregor et al. 2021). Traditionally, it has been argued that industrialization – and the role of the manufacturing sector – has been a key driver of aggregate performance and development, due to the special properties of this sector (e.g., innovative, capital-intensive, high-income elasticity of demand, etc.). Indeed, the set of currently high-income

DOI: 10.4324/9781003590330-3

economies (with few exceptions – e.g., oil states) all had significant shares of both employment and value-added in manufacturing during their transition to high-income status. Recently, it has been observed that many developing and emerging economies are skipping the manufacturing stage, with employment moving from agriculture toward services rather than manufacturing. Such observations have raised the question of whether services can play the role that manufacturing traditionally played and whether premature deindustrialization is likely to limit development opportunities (Felipe et al. 2019).

This chapter uses the information in the Innovation and Structural Transformation Database (Foster-McGregor et al. 2024a, 2024b) to discuss labor productivity and structural change performance and developments across Asia during the last two decades. Specifically, the indicators used out of the full list provided in Chapter 1, Table A1, are as follows (file *DB_Structural_ Change_ProductivityGrowth.xlsx*): Labor productivity index; Labor productivity in 1000s, 2005 US$ per worker; Relative sectoral productivity; Employment share; Value Added; Productivity growth; WS; SSRE; DSRE.

The chapter begins by considering the heterogeneous developments in terms of labor productivity growth across Asia, before identifying the relative roles of within-sector productivity improvements and structural change. Those Asian economies that have performed relatively well in the recent period are those that have been able to generate high within-sector productivity growth rates and those that have been able to shift employment toward more dynamic sectors.[1]

3.2   Labor Productivity Growth Across Asia Has Been Unequal

The Innovation and Structural Transformation Database reports information on aggregate labor productivity developments for the period 1991–2019. In this chapter, we use data for the period 2000–2019. Figure 3.1 reports the level of labor productivity in 2000 and the annual average growth rate of labor productivity during 2000–2019, for all Asian countries in the database, and the USA and Germany as reference countries.

The figure reveals wide variation in initial levels (year 2000) of aggregate labor productivity. Labor productivity is relatively high for Japan, South Korea, Hong Kong, Singapore, Brunei Darussalam, the USA, and Germany, in 2000. In contrast, Myanmar, Cambodia, Afghanistan, and Nepal, among others, reported relatively low initial labor productivity levels.[2] This heterogeneity has important implications for overall economic performance. Considering labor productivity over time, there appears to be evidence of absolute convergence in labor productivity levels, that is, those economies with initially high levels of labor productivity are those that registered the weakest growth rates of labor productivity. The economy with the lowest initial level of labor productivity, Myanmar, was the one that attained the highest growth rate over the period 2000–2019.

Figure 3.2 further indicates that there is a strong positive association between the growth rate of manufacturing labor productivity and aggregate labor

Labor Productivity and Structural Transformation in Asia 29

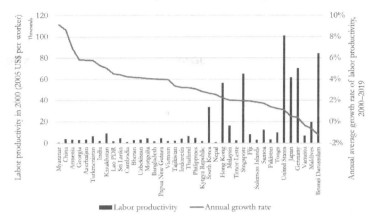

Figure 3.1 Initial Productivity Levels and Growth Rates of Aggregate Labor Productivity, 2000–2019

Note: Countries are organized by growth of labor productivity from highest to lowest.

Source: Authors based on information from the Innovation and Structural Transformation Database

productivity growth for the Asian economies (reference countries the USA and Germany are not included in the graph). The correlation coefficient between these two variables is 0.65. A one percentage point increase in manufacturing labor productivity growth is associated with approximately a 0.3 percentage

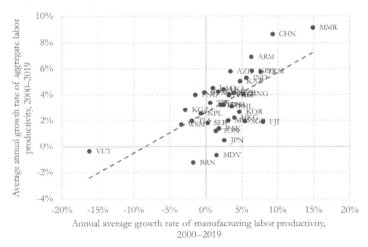

Figure 3.2 Correlation between Labor Productivity Growth in Manufacturing and Aggregate Labor Productivity Growth, 2000–2019

Note: Dotted line is the line of best fit.

Source: Authors based on information from the Innovation and Structural Transformation Database

point increase in aggregate labor productivity growth (this is the slope of the trendline). While a positive relationship could be expected – since manufacturing labor productivity growth is a component of aggregate labor productivity growth – the important aspect is that the positive association is strong, especially since manufacturing employment comprised, on average, just 11% of total employment in 2007 (about the middle of the 2000–2019 period).

3.3 Within-Sector Labor Productivity Growth Differences Explain Most of the Differences in Aggregate Labor Productivity Growth

The Innovation and Structural Transformation Database further allows to examine the broad drivers of aggregate labor productivity growth, in particular whether aggregate productivity developments are due to improvements in productivity within sectors or due to shifts of employment across sectors – what is termed structural change.

More specifically, the database decomposes aggregate labor productivity growth into three terms, namely: (i) within-sector labor productivity growth, capturing improvements within sectors under the assumption that economic structure doesn't change over time; (ii) a static structural change term, with positive values for this term indicating a movement of labor toward sectors that had an initially relatively high level of labor productivity; and (iii) a dynamic structural change effect, for which a positive number would indicate a movement of labor toward sectors that had relatively high labor productivity growth rates over the period under consideration. Box 3.1 provides the technical details.

The results of this productivity decomposition for 2000–2019 are reported in Figure 3.3. They indicate that for most economies – and irrespective of their

---

Box 3.1 Decomposition of Total Labor Productivity Growth into the Within Effect and the Structural Change Effects (Shift-Share Method)

The shift-share method decomposes the growth rate of labor productivity into three components:

- the contribution from changes in the reallocation of labor between sectors, weighted by the initial value of labor productivity (positive if sectors of high productivity increase their employment share, and negative if they decrease their employment shares) – termed the "static structural change effect";

- the interaction between changes in labor productivity and labor shares in individual sectors – termed the "dynamic structural change effect"; and
- the contribution of productivity growth within each sector, weighted by the initial share of each sector in total employment – termed the "within effect."

Algebraically (with each term ordered in the sum), this is expressed as:

$$\pi_N = \frac{\pi_{N,t} - \pi_{N,t-n}}{\pi_{N,t-n}}$$

$$= \frac{\sum_{i=1}^{N} \pi_{i,t-n}\left(S_{i,t} - S_{i,t-n}\right) + \sum_{i=1}^{N}\left(\pi_{i,t} - \pi_{i,t-n}\right)\left(S_{i,t} - S_{i,t-n}\right) + \sum_{i=1}^{N}\left(\pi_{i,t} - \pi_{i,t-n}\right)S_{i,t-n}}{\pi_{N,t-n}},$$

where π is labor productivity, $t - n$ is the initial year, t is the final year, N is the number of sectors, i corresponds to each economic sector, and s is each sector's weight in employment.

Source: Authors

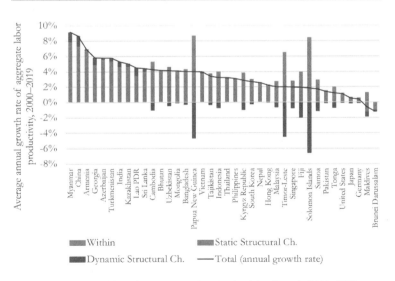

Figure 3.3 Decomposition of Aggregate Labor Productivity Growth, 2000–2019

Note: Vanuatu was dropped from this figure. The data indicate low productivity growth rates for this economy, but with extremely large static and dynamic structural change effects that essentially offset each other. To make the figure more visible for the remaining economies, this economy was dropped from the figure.

Source: Authors based on information from the Innovation and Structural Transformation Database

32 Innovation and Structural Transformation in Asia

overall labor productivity growth rates – the within component was the major driver of productivity growth. In other words, improvements in productivity within sectors (due to technological change and possibly structural change at a finer level of aggregation than used in the database) were the major driver of labor productivity growth for most economies. Structural change was relatively important for some economies, particularly the static structural change term. This is true for Lao PDR, Cambodia, Bangladesh, Papua New Guinea, Indonesia, and Vietnam, among others. The dynamic structural change term plays a positive role in just a few economies, notably Myanmar, China, Georgia, and Lao PDR. In a number of cases, the dynamic structural change term was actually negative (e.g., Papua New Guinea, Timor-Leste, Solomon Islands), indicating that it dragged down overall labor productivity growth, with structural change in these economies occurring toward the less dynamic sectors of the economy.

The database provides information for seven sectors. This allows us to decompose the within effect into the sum of the seven sectoral contributions. Results are reported in Figure 3.4. This figure shows a great deal of variation in the sectoral contributions to the within effect across countries. In many economies, within-sector productivity growth in agriculture was an important contributor. Across the sample of economies, Agriculture accounts for 26% of the (simple) average of within productivity growth. Other sectors are also found to be important across a broad range of countries, in particular Manufacturing (which accounts for 21% of the simple average of the within effect), and Other Activities (which accounts for 24% of the simple average of the within effect).

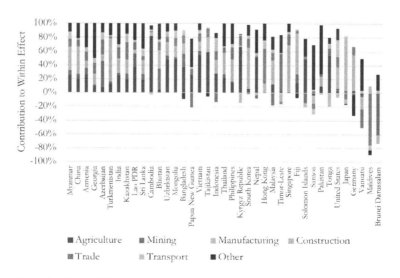

Figure 3.4 Sectoral Contributions to the Within Effect

Source: Authors based on information from the Innovation and Structural Transformation Database

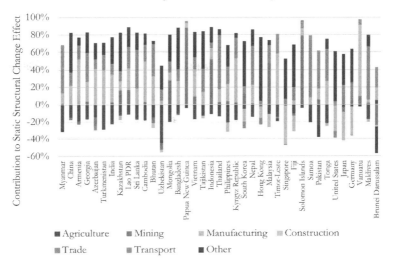

Figure 3.5 Sectoral Contribution to the Static Structural Change Effect

Source: Authors based on information from the Innovation and Structural Transformation Database

Similarly, the two structural change components (static and dynamic effects) (see Box 3.1) can also be decomposed into the sectors' contributions to each. It should be mentioned that the interpretation of the structural change terms is somewhat more complicated since a reduction in the employment share of one sector implies an increase in the share of at least one other. Considering sectors in isolation, therefore, is less meaningful.

Figure 3.5 reports results for the static structural change effect. The static structural change decomposition allows us to identify which sectors have experienced an increase or decrease in their employment shares. Figure 3.5 shows that in nearly all economies there was a shift of employment out of Agriculture over the period 2000–2019. Conversely, Construction provided a positive contribution in most economies, as did Trade, Transport, and Other Activities. Interestingly, in economies with the weakest productivity growth (i.e., economies on the right side of the figure), Manufacturing contributes negatively, suggesting a movement of resources out of manufacturing.

Finally, Figure 3.6 reports the sectoral contributions to the dynamic structural change effect. The interpretation of this figure is the most complex since a positive contribution to the overall dynamic effect of a sector could be due to an increase in both productivity and the sectoral share over time, or due to a decrease in both productivity and the sectoral share over time. Similarly, a negative contribution could be driven by a positive productivity change and a fall in the sectoral share, or by a negative productivity change and a rise in the sectoral share. Despite these difficulties, the figure is somewhat consistent with the figure for the within effect, that is, a negative contribution of Agriculture and positive contributions of Construction, Trade, Transport, and Other Activities,

34 Innovation and Structural Transformation in Asia

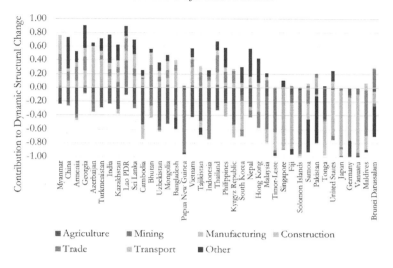

Figure 3.6 Sectoral Contribution to Dynamic Structural Change Effect
Source: Authors based on information from the Innovation and Structural Transformation Database

across many economies. Manufacturing further contributes negatively to many of the worst performing economies in terms of productivity growth.

Summing up the recent performance over the period 2000–2019 of the Asian economies in terms of productivity growth indicates that (i) labor productivity levels across them varied significantly; (ii) there has been convergence in labor productivity; and (iii) structural transformation, measured in terms of the contributions to overall labor productivity growth of the within and employment reallocation growth effects, varies significantly across countries though its effect is usually relatively small. Despite this, there are three facts that characterize labor productivity growth. First, the within effect tends to account for the largest share of overall productivity growth. Second, the static effect is more important than the dynamic effect, with the latter effect contributing negatively – on average – to overall productivity growth across the Asian economies. Third, Agriculture has played an important role in many economies in driving productivity growth, firstly through a relatively high productivity growth rate, and secondly through a reallocation of employment out of this relatively low-productivity sector toward more productive sectors.

3.4 China and Vietnam Present Contrasting Developments in Productivity Performance

China and Vietnam present interesting dynamics in terms of labor productivity growth performance and the relative roles of within-sector productivity growth and structural change in driving overall labor productivity growth. Labor productivity

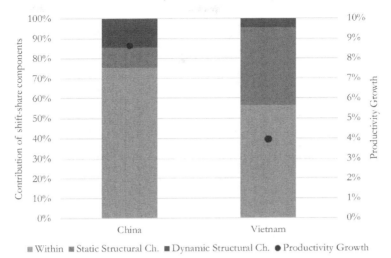

Figure 3.7 Labor Productivity Growth and Its Components, China and Vietnam

Source: Authors based on information from the Innovation and Structural Transformation Database

growth in China was the second highest among the economies covered in the database, with an annual rate of 8.7% over the period 2000–2019 (see Figure 3.7). Conversely, Vietnam registered a much lower rate of labor productivity growth, at just 4.0% per annum. In the case of China, within-sector labor productivity growth accounted for around 75% of overall labor productivity growth, while for Vietnam, this share was about 50%. The productivity-enhancing structural change that did take place in China was predominantly due to dynamic structural change. For Vietnam, structural change played a larger role in driving overall labor productivity growth, but this structural change tended to be of the static type.

Using information on sectoral productivity growth rates and changes in the economic structure, it is possible to further understand the different productivity dynamics of the two economies. Ultimately, these two dimensions – sectoral productivity and sectoral structure – allow for the construction of the productivity growth decomposition.

Given the relative importance of the within effect in overall productivity growth, Figure 3.8 reports information on the sectoral contributions to the within effect in both China and Vietnam. It is noticeable that Agriculture contributed over 50% of the overall within effect in Vietnam, while it contributed less than 20% in China. Conversely, manufacturing contributed almost 40% of the within effect in China, but less than 15% in Vietnam. Similarly, Other Activities contributed significantly more to the within effect in China than in Vietnam (22% versus 9%). In sum, the drivers of the within effect in China tended to be Manufacturing, Other Activities, and Transport and Communication Services, while in Vietnam it was Agriculture.

36 *Innovation and Structural Transformation in Asia*

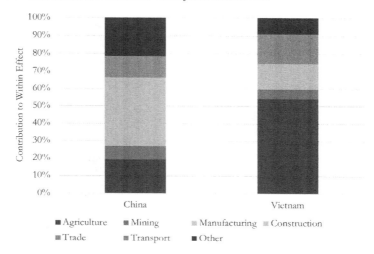

Figure 3.8 Sectoral Contributions to the Within-Sector Productivity Growth Effect, China and Vietnam

Source: Authors based on information from the Innovation and Structural Transformation Database

To understand the drivers of the within effect further, Figures 3.9 and 3.10 report information on the initial (i.e., year 2000) employment share and the change in sectoral labor productivity between 2000 and 2019, relative to the initial aggregate labor productivity, for China and Vietnam, respectively. These two terms combined (multiplied) define the within effect.

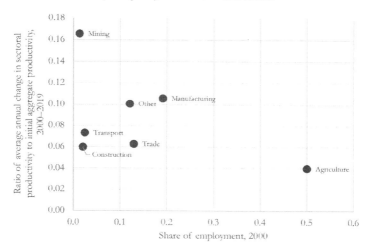

Figure 3.9 Scatterplot of Initial Employment Shares and the Change in Relative Labor Productivity, China, 2000–2019

Source: Authors based on information from the Innovation and Structural Transformation Database

Labor Productivity and Structural Transformation in Asia 37

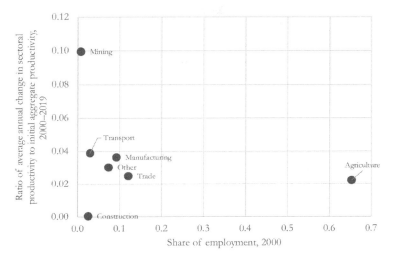

Figure 3.10 Scatterplot of Initial Employment Shares and the Change in Relative Labor Productivity, Vietnam, 2000–2019

Source: Authors based on information from the Innovation and Structural Transformation Database

In the case of China (Figure 3.9), we observe a large initial employment share of Agriculture (50%), with Manufacturing having a share of 19%, Trade of 13%, and Other Activities of 12%. The remaining sectors have initial employment shares below 5%. While the highest employment share is that of Agriculture, it also had the lowest change in relative labor productivity, with this change being particularly large in Mining, and to a lesser extent in Manufacturing and Other Activities. Combined, these results explain the within effect. Agriculture made a strong contribution to the within effect because of its share in overall employment, despite registering low labor productivity growth. Conversely, Manufacturing and to a lesser extent Other Activities contributed the most to the within effect because of their relatively high labor productivity growth over the period and because of their relatively high employment shares.

Results for Vietnam (Figure 3.10) show somewhat similar patterns, with Agriculture having the highest initial employment share and Mining the highest growth rate of labor productivity. Indeed, the share of Agriculture in initial employment is even higher in the case of Vietnam (65%). This high share results in Agriculture making the greatest contribution to the within effect, despite having the second lowest labor productivity growth (2.7%). The small role of Manufacturing in the within effect can also be explained by this figure, with Manufacturing having a relatively small share of initial employment (9%) and a change in relative labor productivity (5.1%) that was not significantly different from that in most other sectors, including Agriculture.

Figures 3.11 and 3.12 provide information about the change in sectoral employment shares between 2000 and 2019 and the ratio of sectoral labor productivity to aggregate-level productivity in the initial period.

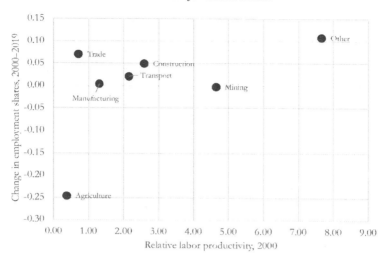

Figure 3.11 Scatterplot of Sectoral Labor Productivity and the Change in Employment Shares, China, 2000–2019

Source: Authors based on information from the Innovation and Structural Transformation Database

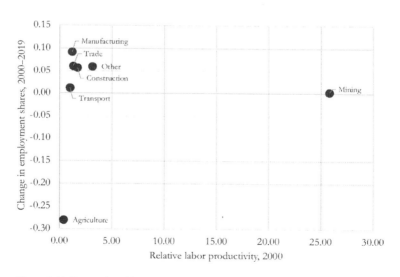

Figure 3.12 Scatterplot of Sectoral Labor Productivity and the Change in Employment Shares, Vietnam, 2000–2019

Source: Authors based on information from the Innovation and Structural Transformation Database

Combined, these two pieces of information provide information about the importance of different sectors in driving the overall between or structural change effect.

The results for China (Figure 3.11) highlight why the structural change effect was limited in China. With the exception of Other Activities, the sectors with the highest relative labor productivity are also those that saw little or no change in employment shares over time. This is true for Mining and Manufacturing, and to a lesser extent for Transport and Construction. The structural change that did occur was from Agriculture to Other Activities, Trade, and, to a lesser extent, Construction. With the exception of Other Activities, these are sectors with relatively low labor productivity levels, meaning that structural-change-driven labor productivity growth was quite weak.

Results for Vietnam (Figure 3.12) are to a large extent similar to those for China, with a large drop in the employment share of Agriculture observed and little change in the employment share of Mining. There was a relatively large shift of employment toward Manufacturing in Vietnam, with shifts also toward Trade, Other Activities, and Construction. The relative productivity of these sectors is not much higher than that in Agriculture, however, suggesting that these movements of employment will not have large impacts on overall labor productivity growth. At the same time, the relatively small contribution of within-sector productivity growth in Vietnam, relative to China's, means that the structural change term played a relatively large role in Vietnam. While our database is not able to explain the differential productivity levels and growth rates within sectors that have driven the different dynamics of the within-sector contribution, it is likely that such differences arose as a result of higher levels of investment and capital intensity, differences in the technological sophistication of sectors, and a more optimal allocation of resources within sectors (e.g., across firms or more disaggregated sectors).

Notes

1 A previous analysis of Asia's economic transformation is provided by the Asian Development Bank (2013).
2 While the data are in constant US dollars, differences in price levels across different countries are not fully captured (e.g., through the use of purchasing power parities). As such, the data are more relevant for an analysis of growth rates and developments within countries across time rather than cross-country comparisons.

4 Recent Developments in Global Value Chains in Asia

4.1 Introduction: Global Value Chains as a Development Paradigm

International trade has long been regarded as a crucial driver of economic growth and development. From a theoretical perspective, a movement from autarky to free trade is expected to lead to a reallocation of resources in line with comparative advantage. This reallocation can lead to a one-off increase in the level of income. Additional static gains may accrue through the reduction in x-inefficiency and rent-seeking behavior that may accompany protectionism (Krueger 1998). The development of endogenous growth models, however, showed the possibility of long-run growth effects from trade (e.g., Romer 1990; Grossman and Helpman 1991). The possibility of monopoly profits in these models provides the incentive for innovation, which generates technological progress and long-run growth. International trade can enhance these incentives by increasing the resources available for innovation and by facilitating the diffusion of knowledge across borders.

Trade is considered to have played a leading role in transforming the economies of several Asian countries since the end of WWII. While many countries in Latin America and Africa adopted import substitution policies as a means of shifting comparative advantage and allowing for industrialization behind protective barriers, countries in Asia are considered to have adopted a more export-oriented approach. Among other factors, the rapid growth in South Korea since the 1960s has been attributed to its export-oriented strategy, with firms having to meet strict export targets. According to Studwell (2013), this approach helped weed out the "losers" – that is, those firms unable to compete on international markets – shifting resources to more competitive firms.

More recently, interest has been focused on the rise of global value chains (GVCs) and their role in facilitating economic growth and development (Taglioni and Winkler 2016). GVCs split up the different activities needed to produce a good or service, with these different activities undertaken in different countries. Their rise has been driven by three main factors. Firstly,

DOI: 10.4324/9781003590330-4

reductions in trade costs due to the rapid liberalization of trade that has occurred since the end of WWII, through both multilateral trade liberalization in the context of the GATT and World Trade Organization and bilateral and plurilateral liberalization in the form of preferential trade agreements. Trade costs have been further reduced by improvements in transport and logistics, including containerization (Bernhofen et al. 2016). Secondly, improvements in information and communication technologies have allowed an easier coordination of activities across borders. Thirdly, differences in factor costs provide the rationale for firms to shift stages of production to those countries in which they can be undertaken most efficiently or cheaply.

GVCs can be considered to represent an extreme form of Adam Smith's concept of the division of labor, with countries specializing in narrow tasks in the production of a good or service. In addition to the potential impacts of trade on growth and development mentioned above, GVCs are considered to offer additional benefits. Baldwin (2011), for example, suggests that GVCs can allow for more rapid industrialization. Arguments favoring the role of GVCs in development have revolved around the idea that, unlike in the past, economies do not need to develop the entire course of production but can instead focus on specific activities within a GVC (such as final assembly or production of some components). This, it is argued, allows for an easier path to development, with China often cited as an example of an economy that has exploited GVCs, with these being an important component of its recent growth performance and development strategy (Dollar 2019).

In integrating into GVCs, China has been able to both enter high-tech value chains, such as electronics, as well as progressively upgrade and diversify within value chains. Upgrading in this sense involves a move along the value chain to positions in which a country can capture more of the value added within value chains, something that often involves a move away from assembly activities toward component production, tasks related to innovation, and downstream post-production tasks, as well as a movement toward more sophisticated value chains. Within Asia, Vietnam appears to be following a similar path by developing capabilities in high-tech value chains. In contrast, Bangladesh has been able to enter GVCs, which has driven economic growth and job creation over the past decade or more, but its integration has been concentrated almost entirely on assembly activities in the ready-made garment sector.

The example of Bangladesh provides some anecdotal support for those who argue that GVC integration can be a hindrance to development by forcing developing countries to specialize in low value-added segments of value chains, where there is little opportunity for upgrading (World Bank and World Trade Organization 2019, Chapter 7). Such discussions highlight the importance of positioning and upgrading in GVCs in determining the developmental effect of GVCs for a country. Identifying sectors and activities within GVCs that allow for the capture of large shares of value added is crucial in maximizing the benefits of GVCs, while upgrading and moving into higher value-added activities that offer innovation opportunities can facilitate dynamics gains from GVC integration, with some evidence that China has been successful in this upgrading (Kee and Tang 2016).

Beyond issues of positioning and upgrading, recent developments have raised questions over whether GVCs can play the role of development escalators and whether they can assist economies to expedite development. One component of this discussion has been the stagnation of GVC activity since the Global Financial Crisis of 2008/2009 (Dachs and Pahl 2019). Explanations for this stagnation are varied and include continued weak demand, new automation technologies that are limiting opportunities for labor-rich countries to participate in GVCs (Stapleton 2019), and weakening support for the GVC model in response to perceived and observed impacts of trade and GVCs on inequality and labor market outcomes in developed countries (Autor et al. 2013).

Concerns around this "slowbalization" or "deglobalization" have risen in response to increased trade tensions between the USA and China specifically, and more broadly, as a result of the rise in the number of protectionist policies implemented. These include policies bundled into broad new industrial strategies across a range of countries that are intended to build and protect domestic production capabilities in key industries, to de-risk and build resilient value chains, and to encourage strategic autonomy. The COVID-19 pandemic and other supply chain disruptions provided an important impetus for these approaches, further increasing discussions over the need for reshoring and nearshoring as a way of mitigating the risk associated with distant and dispersed value chains (Elia et al. 2021). This is despite evidence suggesting that GVCs have been quite resilient to these shocks, recovering rapidly following the pandemic, with those countries more integrated into GVCs recovering more rapidly (Giglioli et al. 2021). Regional value chains and services value chains specifically appear to have shown relatively strong resilience (World Bank and World Trade Organization 2019).

This chapter discusses recent developments in GVC participation across Asian countries and identifies their positioning in GVCs, both regarding the activities they perform and the global or regional nature of their integration. Finally, the chapter focuses on two important and contrasting economies – China and Vietnam – to further understand recent developments in GVC integration.

Building on the arguments above, we highlight two points. Firstly, in the context of recent developments in GVC integration, it is important to measure and monitor the integration of economies into GVCs. Secondly, it is relevant to understand how economies are integrated into GVCs. This latter aspect may include an understanding of the sectors in which economies are integrated in value chains (such as manufacturing versus services chains), the positioning of economies within specific value chains (i.e., identifying the types of activities that economies undertake within value chains), and the global or regional nature of their value chain integration. Developments along these different dimensions are crucial in identifying the opportunities that countries have in using GVCs for development purposes, and in integrating into GVCs in ways that can build resilience to shocks.

The chapter uses the information in the Innovation and Structural Transformation Database (Foster-McGregor et al. 2024a, 2024b) on GVC integration and positioning, across Asia during the last two decades. Specifically, the indicators used out of the full list provided in Chapter 1, Table A1, are as follows (file *DB_GVC_Integration.xlsx*): Backward linkages, foreign share; Forward linkages, foreign share; Backward geo-radius; Forward geo-radius.

4.2 Developments in Asia's GVC Integration and Positioning

The dataset considers two sets of indicators to measure the integration and positioning of economies within GVCs (see Box 4.1). The first reports information on the source of value added used in an economy-sector's final demand. Such value added can come from three sources: from the sector itself,

Box 4.1 Measuring Global Value Chain Participation

The measurement of a country's participation in GVCs relies upon so-called multi-country input-output tables. We use the tables prepared by the Asian Development Bank, which can be accessed through: https://www.adb.org/what-we-do/data/regional-input-output-tables. Below is a stylized example of a multi-country input-output table.

	Australian mining	Indian steel	Chinese bicycles	Global consumer demand	Total output
Australian mining	3	8	0	0	11
Indian steel	0	2	15	0	17
Chinese bicycles	0	0	6	25	31
Payments for labor and capital	8	7	10	–	–
Total output	11	17	31	–	–

The prime unit of analysis in this table is the so-called country-sector combinations, e.g., the mining industry in Australia. The rows of the table represent the deliveries of intermediate goods of the country-sectors to other country sectors, and to final users. Final users are either households or governments. These consume the output of the country-sectors, or (other) country-sectors that produce the final output. All data in the table are in a common currency, e.g., US$. In the example table, the Australian mining sector delivers $8 worth of intermediate goods (e.g., ores) to the Indian steel sector, which delivers $15 intermediates (steel) to the Chinese bicycle sector, which delivers a total of $25 to final users worldwide.

Each row sums to the total output of a country-sector. The columns document the use of a country-sector. For example, the Chinese bicycle sector uses $15 worth of steel from the Indian steel industry, $6 worth of its own intermediates (e.g., parts), and pays $10 for labor (i.e., wages) and the use of capital (i.e., profits). Each column sums up to the same total output as the corresponding row does because profits are calculated as the residual between the value of total output and the country-sector's payments for inputs (intermediates and labor).

GVC analysis as we use it is aimed at accounting for the direct and indirect contributions of all country-sectors that supply value to a value chain. For this purpose, we consider each country-sector as its own global value chain that delivers final output to final users worldwide. In our example table, the Chinese bicycle country-sector is the only one among the three country-sectors that delivers to final demand. Hence, the table can be considered a complete and detailed way of accounting (only) for the Chinese bicycle GVC.

Total value supplied by this GVC is $25 because this is what is supplied to global final users. However, gross output of the GVC is larger than this: summed over the three country-sectors it is $11 + $17 + $31 = $59. However, this contains many double-counts. For a fair representation of where the $25 value of the GVC comes from, we must consider value added, which in this case is the payments of each country-sector for labor and capital, or, alternatively, each country-sector's total output minus its use of intermediates. Summing values added in the three country-sectors, we see indeed that the total ($25) is equal to the value that the chain delivers to final users.

This way of accounting shows that both the Indian steel and Australian mining country-sectors contribute to the final value delivered by the

> Chinese bicycle GVC. Together, these two sectors contribute 60%, or (8+7)/15, of total value delivered by the Chinese bicycle GVC. This way of looking at the GVC is what is called the "backward" perspective: it asks where the value supplied by the Chinese bicycle GVC originated. Alternatively, the "forward" perspective takes the point of view of the delivering country-sectors, in the example Australian mining and Indian steel, which deliver all (100%) of their value to the Chinese bicycle GVC.
>
> However, in real-world multi-country input-output tables, many individual GVCs are aggregated into just one (very large) table. In fact, each of the country-sectors in such a real-world table will have its own GVC. Although the mathematical details of the method that we use for GVC accounting are complicated (and therefore beyond the scope of this box), they can be summarized by saying that what we do is decompose the large real-world table into smaller ones like the example table that we used. Mathematical details of this method can be found in Koopman et al. (2014) and Timmer et al. (2021). Further details of how we applied those principles exactly can be found in Foster-McGregor et al. (2024b).
>
> Thus, the final value delivered by each country-sector is considered a GVC, and we calculate the contribution of all other country-sectors in the big table to the GVC's final value. The foreign component of this is used as our indicator of backward GVC integration. On the other hand, the contribution that each country-sector makes to foreign GVCs, expressed as a percentage of total value added that it produces, is our indicator of forward integration.
>
> Source: Authors

from other sectors within the economy of interest, and from foreign sources. The second set of indicators provides information on the destination of an economy-sector's value added, which again has three destinations: the same sector, other domestic sectors, or sectors in other economies. This chapter considers the share of value added supplied to a sector from foreign sources as an indicator of GVC integration. This captures backward linkages in GVCs. Higher values of this indicator imply that final demand in a country-sector contains a relatively large share of value added from third economies, suggesting that this economy-sector is engaged into activities such as assembly within GVCs, which require inputs from other countries.

46 *Innovation and Structural Transformation in Asia*

The chapter further uses the share of value added of an economy-sector that is embodied in foreign final demand. This is an indicator of forward integration into GVCs. This indicator captures the extent to which a country-sector is engaged in GVCs as a supplier of intermediate goods, raw materials, and service inputs to third economies, with higher values of this indicator indicating that the country-sector is intensive in activities that serve other economies' final production activities. The database reports these and other indicators for the period 2007–2019.

One challenge in identifying a country's trade openness – including its integration in GVCs – is that larger countries do not need to specialize to the same extent as smaller countries. This means that while larger countries will tend to report higher trade values, when considering indicators of trade openness expressed relative to some indicator of a country's size, larger countries will tend to report smaller values. To overcome this challenge, Figures 4.1 and 4.2 report the values of backward and forward integration in GVCs in 2019, respectively, along with the level of GDP (in constant PPP$). Also reported is a line of best fit. Countries above this line can, therefore, be considered to have levels of GVC integration higher than expected given their income levels, while those below would have lower levels of GVC integration than expected given income levels.

In terms of backward linkages within GVCs (Figure 4.1), the levels of backward GVC integration confirm the negative relationship between GVC integration and income levels, with larger countries such as China, India, and

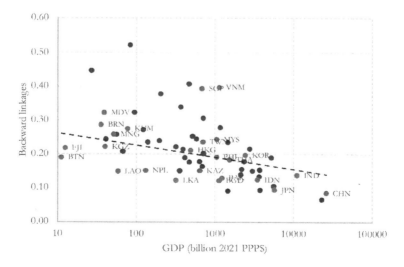

Figure 4.1 Backward GVC Integration in 2019 by GDP Levels

Note: Dotted line is the line of best fit.

Source: Authors based on information from the Innovation and Structural Transformation Database and World Development Indicators

Japan reporting relatively low levels of backward GVC integration. Smaller countries like Singapore or Maldives report much higher levels. When controlling for income levels, however, it can be observed that many Asian countries are integrated into GVCs through backward linkages at a level consistent with their size. Economies including India, Hong Kong, Thailand, and South Korea have backward integration levels that are roughly in line with what would be expected given their size. The Asian countries that report high values of backward integration, conditional on their size, are Singapore and Vietnam, with Malaysia also showing relatively high values. In contrast, a set of South Asian (Bangladesh, Nepal, Pakistan, Sri Lanka) and Central Asian (Kazakhstan, Kyrgyz Republic, Mongolia) countries show lower than expected levels of backward GVC integration, with Japan also reporting relatively low levels. The results highlight that very few countries in Asia are integrated into GVCs through backward linkages to an extent greater than would be predicted by their size.

A strong negative relationship between country size and forward GVC linkages is shown in Figure 4.2, with China, India, and Japan again reporting relatively low values of GVC integration in 2019. In the case of forward linkages, however, there is greater deviation of Asian countries from the predicted levels of integration. Several countries report levels of GVC integration higher than expected. This again includes Singapore, Vietnam, and Malaysia. Brunei Darussalam, Mongolia, and Kazakhstan are also included in this group, highlighting their role as suppliers of raw materials in GVCs. South

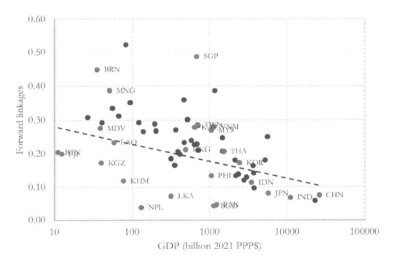

Figure 4.2 Forward GVC Integration in 2019 by GDP Levels

Note: Dotted line is the line of best fit.

Source: Authors based on information from the Innovation and Structural Transformation Database and World Development Indicators

48 *Innovation and Structural Transformation in Asia*

Asian countries (Bangladesh, India, Maldives, Nepal, Pakistan, Sri Lanka) are generally found to be integrated into GVCs through forward linkages to a lesser extent than expected. Finally, some Southeast Asian (Cambodia, Indonesia, Lao PDR, the Philippines) countries also report relatively low levels of forward integration.

These results provide important initial insights. They show that some countries have been able to integrate into GVCs to a greater extent than predicted by their size. Singapore, Vietnam, and Malaysia report relatively high values of both backward and forward linkages, while others report relatively high values for forward GVC linkages, highlighting their role as raw material and intermediate suppliers in GVCs. Others have been unsuccessful in integrating. This is the case of South Asian countries, integrated to a lesser extent than expected in both forward and backward linkages in GVCs. Southeast Asian countries show relatively weak performance in forward linkages in GVCs. Economies that are often considered to have strongly integrated into GVCs (e.g., China, Hong Kong, Thailand) are found to be integrated in GVCs at about what is predicted by their size. The observed differences in results for forward and backward linkages further suggest that the positioning countries take in GVCs can be important.

A comparison of the backward and forward integration measures provides insights into the relative positioning of countries within GVCs, with Figure 4.3 reporting the relative importance of backward and forward GVC integration (i.e., the share of total GVC integration due to either backward or forward linkages) in 2019. The figure indicates significant differences in positioning across Asian economies. Consistent with the findings above,

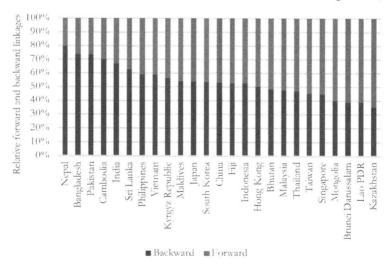

Figure 4.3 Relative Backward and Forward Linkages in 2019

Source: Authors based on information from the Innovation and Structural Transformation Database

Kazakhstan (due to mining) has relatively high values of forward integration, as do economies such as Taiwan, Singapore, and Hong Kong (due to services inputs and parts and components production). Conversely, countries such as Bangladesh, India, Pakistan, and Vietnam have relatively high values of the backward integration indicator, suggesting that these economies are more strongly integrated into GVCs through assembly type activities.

The concept of the "smile curve" suggests that countries that can integrate both upstream and downstream in GVCs can benefit by capturing a greater share of the value added in production (World Trade Organization 2021, Chapter 1). This simple argument neglects the range of activities that can take place at either end of the value chain. Moreover, the use of indicators based on input-output data cannot consider the post-sales activities that often include high value-added downstream activities. In the case of forward linkages and upstream activities, the examples highlighted above provide an interesting comparison. For example, Hong Kong, Taiwan, and Singapore have been able to integrate upstream in relatively high-tech components production, most notably microchips in the case of Taiwan. In contrast, countries such as Kazakhstan have integrated through the extraction and export of raw materials. These represent very different types of integration: the former by relying on and building domestic capabilities and innovative activities, while the latter by exploiting a natural resource. The potential for long-term growth and development will be affected by how countries specialize in GVCs. In the case of natural resource-based integration, there is a need to diversify into other activities to help build the domestic capabilities needed for long-run growth. This is one justification for Indonesia's export ban on nickel, for example, a ban intended to help shift domestic production towards more downstream processing activities. At the other end, countries with high backward linkages and downstream GVC activity face a similar set of risks to natural resource producers. There is a risk that such countries become stuck in the assembly of low-tech manufacturing goods, again limiting their ability to improve domestic capabilities and upgrade in value chains. A more balanced and diversified integration into GVCs, such as that of China, perhaps represents the best opportunity for upgrading and increasing the domestic capture of value added in value chains, therefore.

As a means of highlighting the dynamics of GVC integration in Asia, Figure 4.4 combines information on the changes in backward and forward GVC integration between 2007 and 2019. The figure reveals a great deal of heterogeneity in GVC integration dynamics, with economies appearing in all four quadrants. In quadrant IV, a set of economies (including the Philippines, Pakistan, Hong Kong, and Nepal) have experienced increases in backward GVC integration alongside declines in forward GVC integration, suggesting

50 Innovation and Structural Transformation in Asia

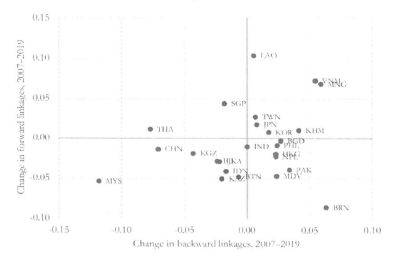

Figure 4.4 Changes in Forward and Backward Linkages Between 2007 and 2019
Source: Authors based on information from the Innovation and Structural Transformation Database

a movement towards more final assembly type activities. In the case of Nepal and Pakistan, this change comes despite these economies already having relatively high backward linkages. In quadrant II, Thailand and Singapore experienced rising forward integration and falling backward integration, suggesting a movement toward the increased supply of raw materials, and services inputs, parts and components. These two sets of economies, therefore, have seen strong shifts in their positioning within GVCs, with one dimension of GVC integration and positioning increasing at the expense of the other. These represent a diverse set of countries and circumstances, with some increasing forward GVC activity in extractive sectors and others in parts and components production. As discussed above, these present different development opportunities. There is a further set of economies – including South Korea, Vietnam, and Cambodia – which have experienced increases across both dimensions of GVC integration, suggesting a deeper integration into GVCs more generally (quadrant I). Finally, there are a set of economies that includes China, Indonesia, and Sri Lanka that have seen declines in both dimensions of GVC integration (quadrant III). The causes of these declines are likely diverse, with geopolitics and increasing trade tensions being one factor. Other factors may include domestic policies and deteriorating domestic economic performance.

An important question is whether integration into GVCs has allowed economies to upgrade within them. While there are various definitions and dimensions of upgrading, one approach is to consider the share of value

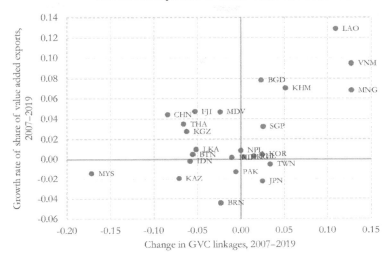

Figure 4.5 Growth in the Contribution of Value Added to Global Exports and Change in GVC Integration, 2007–2019

Source: Authors based on information from the Innovation and Structural Transformation Database

added in global exports as a means of identifying the extent to which economies capture the gains from value chains. An economy can increase its share of value added either by increasing the scale of its activities within GVCs or by moving toward activities that capture a higher share of value added.

Figure 4.5 graphs the growth rate of the share of an economy in global value-added exports against the change in the level of GVC integration (as measured by the sum of forward and backward GVC integration), between 2007 and 2019. The figure reveals that except for a small number of countries (including Japan, Kazakhstan, Malaysia, Pakistan, and Taiwan), Asian countries have been able to increase their share of value added in global exports, suggesting widespread upgrading (according to this definition).

Developments in levels of GVC integration have been more diverse, however, with China and Vietnam highlighting this diversity. Both countries have seen increases in their share of value added in global exports, but in the case of China, this was in the context of declining GVC integration, while in the case of Vietnam, GVC integration increased. These different dynamics provide some support for the idea that China was able to upgrade by increasing its domestic share of value added in its production (and thus decreasing the foreign share), while Vietnam has been able to increase its share in value added in global exports by expanding the scale of its production and exports, albeit with a high share of this increase due to foreign value added.

4.3 The Changing Geography of Global Value Chains

To examine developments in the geographical scope of GVCs, novel indicators of the GVC radius are calculated. The backward GVC radius measures the weighted average distance to foreign suppliers, with the weights being the value-added contributions of other countries to final demand in the country of interest. Conversely, the forward GVC radius measures the weighted average distance to countries supplied by the country of interest, with the weights being the share of value added supplied to other countries by the country of interest. Both indicators are then normalized to lie between zero and one, with higher numbers implying a greater radius. Higher numbers are therefore associated with a more global focus of GVCs, while lower numbers suggest a focus on more regional value chains.

Figures 4.6 and 4.7 report information on the 2007 value of the backward and forward radius, respectively, along with the change in this radius between 2007 and 2019. In terms of backward GVC integration, economies such as Singapore, Mongolia, Brunei Darussalam, Bangladesh, and Hong Kong appear to be the most globally integrated, while economies such as Fiji, Cambodia, Vietnam, Nepal, Taiwan, and Lao PDR appear to be more regionally integrated into GVCs. Of perhaps more interest than the absolute numbers are the changes over time, with most economies witnessing declines in the backward integration radius. These declines are relatively large in Mongolia, Brunei Darussalam, Bhutan, and Lao PDR. Indeed, only in three economies (China, Malaysia, and Fiji) do we observe increases in the backward integration radius.

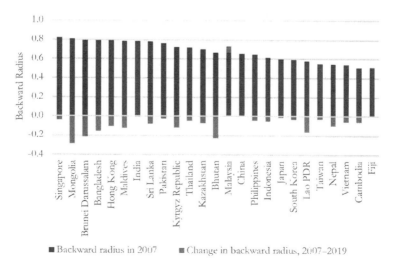

Figure 4.6 Backward Radius in 2007 and Changes in the Backward Radius Between 2007 and 2019

Source: Authors based on information from the Innovation and Structural Transformation Database

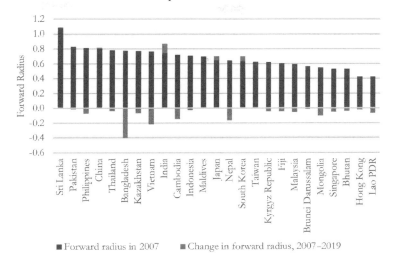

Figure 4.7 Forward Radius in 2007 and Changes in the Forward Radius Between 2007 and 2019

Source: Authors based on information from the Innovation and Structural Transformation Database

Figure 4.7 reports the radius for forward GVC integration, with the results suggesting a quite different ranking from that in Figure 4.6. Certain economies that had a high backward integration radius report a relatively low forward integration radius. Examples of these economies are Hong Kong, Singapore, Brunei Darussalam, and Malaysia. On average, these economies tend to be more globally integrated in terms of their backward GVC integration, but more regionally integrated in terms of forward GVC integration. In other words, they rely more globally for sourcing intermediate goods but have a more regional focus in their supplying activities. Other countries appear to have relatively high values of both indicators of integration radius, examples being Sri Lanka, Pakistan, and Bangladesh. Once again, observing changes over time, the forward integration radius declined in most economies, indicating that value chain integration has become more regional. There are again exceptions to this rule, however, with economies such as China, India, Japan, South Korea, and Sri Lanka seeing increases in the forward GVC radius, often from initially relatively high levels.

Combining information on the changes in the forward and backward radius over time, Figure 4.8 reveals that in only one economy – China – did both radii increase. In most other countries, a decline in both radii was observed. There are also several cases where the radius along one dimension increased and that along the other dimension declined. In the cases of Fiji and Malaysia, increases in the backward radius are observed alongside declines in the forward radius. Conversely, in the Maldives, Sri Lanka, South Korea, Japan, and India, increases in the forward radius are combined with reductions in the backward radius.

54 *Innovation and Structural Transformation in Asia*

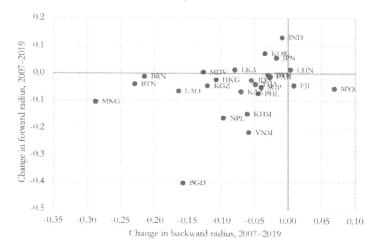

Figure 4.8 Changes in Forward and Backward Radius, 2007–2019

Source: Authors based on information from the Innovation and Structural Transformation Database

Identifying the reasons for the regionalization of Asia's GVC activity is not straightforward. This may be a result of increased regional cooperation and integration through the formation of trade agreements. Alternatively, it may represent a response to increased geopolitical tensions and involve some form of nearshoring within Asia. The potential consequences of this regionalization are also unclear. To the extent that regionalization reflects the rise of multinationals as well as lead GVC firms from the region, this may represent a positive change that could help integrate into GVCs Asian countries that have struggled to enter them to date. Conversely, if the trend toward detaching from other parts of the world limits the flow of knowledge, technology, and capital, the long-run developmental effects could be negative.

4.4 Divergent Trends – The Case of China and Vietnam

As documented above, recent developments in the performance of the Asian economies in terms of GVC integration have been mixed. China and Vietnam represent two extreme – albeit related – situations, with GVC integration diminishing along both the forward and backward dimension in the case of China, and GVC integration increasing along both dimensions in the case of Vietnam. We now delve into the relative performance of these two cases.

4.4.1 *Sectoral Drivers of Divergent Trends*

Figures 4.9 and 4.10 report information on developments in backward and forward GVC integration for China at the sectoral level, with the Innovation and Structural Transformation Database reporting data for 35 sectors. In particular, the figures report information for the 2007 levels of backward and forward

Recent Developments in Global Value Chains in Asia 55

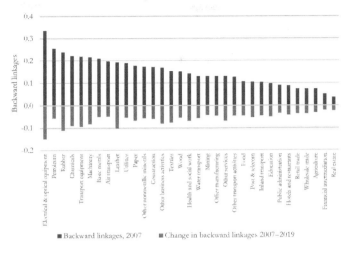

Figure 4.9 Sectoral Backward GVC Integration in 2007 and Changes Between 2007 and 2019 in China

Source: Authors based on information from the Innovation and Structural Transformation Database

integration and the change in these levels between 2007 and 2019. In the case of China, large values of backward integration (Figure 4.9) are observed in 2007 for Electrical and Optical equipment especially, highlighting the role of China as an assembler in this sector. Relatively high values of backward integration

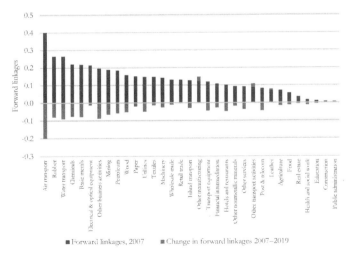

Figure 4.10 Sectoral Forward GVC Integration in 2007 and Changes Between 2007 and 2019 in China

Source: Authors based on information from the Innovation and Structural Transformation Database

are also observed in sectors such as Rubber, Chemicals, and Machinery, among others. Considering changes over time, declines in the level of backward integration are observed across all sectors, with the declines being relatively large in the case of Electrical and Optical equipment, Rubber, and Leather.

Turning to forward integration (Figure 4.10), relatively large values in 2007 were observed in Air Transport, Rubber, Water Transport, and Chemicals, among others. With few exceptions, there were declines in the level of forward integration over time, declines that tended to be larger in those sectors that had the highest initial values. Combined, the results suggest that China has seen declines in both forward and backward GVC integration, declines that occurred across a broad set of sectors.

The case of Vietnam is somewhat different. In terms of backward integration (Figure 4.11), Vietnam had relatively high levels across several sectors, including Petroleum, Electrical and Optical equipment, Water Transport, Leather, and Transport equipment, among others. Over time, however, there were increases in backward GVC integration in many sectors. Such increases were relatively large in Paper, Health and Social work, Air Transport, and Post, among others. There were declines in backward integration in certain sectors, particularly those sectors with the highest initial levels of backward integration.

Turning to forward integration (Figure 4.12), Vietnam reports high forward linkages in many primary and raw materials-intensive sectors such as Mining, Rubber, and Wood, with relatively low values in many other sectors. There have been increases in forward integration across a broad range of sectors, however, with increases being particularly large in electrical and optical equipment, basic metals, and transport equipment.

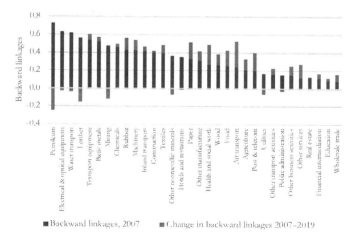

Figure 4.11 Sectoral Backward GVC Integration in 2007 and Changes Between 2007 and 2019 in Vietnam

Source: Authors based on information from the Innovation and Structural Transformation Database

Recent Developments in Global Value Chains in Asia 57

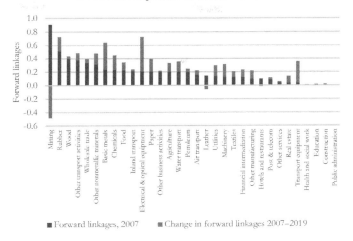

Figure 4.12 Sectoral Forward GVC Integration in 2007 and Changes Between 2007 and 2019 in Vietnam

Source: Authors based on information from the Innovation and Structural Transformation Database

4.4.2 Geographical Drivers of Divergent Trends

In addition to the change in the forward and backward positioning in GVCs, the two countries have witnessed divergent developments in the extent of regional and global value chain integration. Figures 4.13 and 4.14 report the initial values of the backward and forward GVC radius in 2007 for China, respectively, along

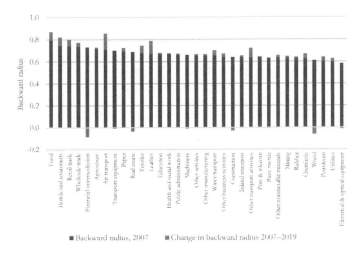

Figure 4.13 Sectoral Backward Radius in 2007 and Change Between 2007 and 2019 in China

Source: Authors based on information from the Innovation and Structural Transformation Database

58 Innovation and Structural Transformation in Asia

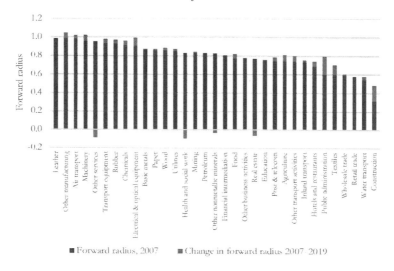

Figure 4.14 Sectoral Forward Radius in 2007 and Change Between 2007 and 2019 in China
Source: Authors based on information from the Innovation and Structural Transformation Database

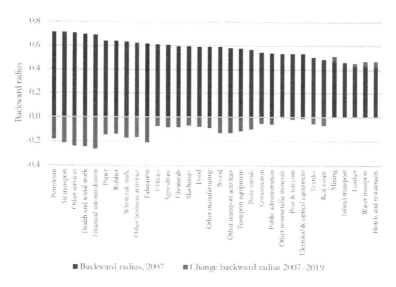

Figure 4.15 Sectoral Backward Radius in 2007 and Change Between 2007 and 2019 in the Vietnam
Source: Authors based on information from the Innovation and Structural Transformation Database

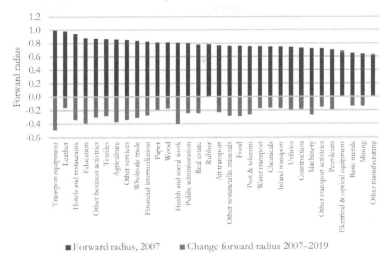

Figure 4.16 Sectoral Forward Radius in 2007 and Change Between 2007 and 2019 in the Vietnam

Source: Authors based on information from the Innovation and Structural Transformation Database

with the change in these indicators between 2007 and 2019. The figures indicate that across a broad range of sectors, there has been an increase in both the backward and forward GVC radii, with declines being limited to a small number of services sectors (e.g., Financial intermediation, Real estate activities) and low-tech manufacturing sectors (e.g., Wood, Other non-metallic minerals).

Figures 4.15 and 4.16 report the same information for Vietnam. Here, the developments are in stark contrast to those of China. Strong declines in the GVC backward radius are observed across almost all sectors, with similarly large declines observed for the forward radius, except for Rubber, Electrical and Optical Equipment, and Other Manufacturing, where the changes were positive but minimal. Declines in the radius tend to be larger for those sectors with initially high levels – and therefore sectors that were relatively globally integrated in value chains – particularly in the case of the backward radius. Overall, the results across sectors suggest a strong regionalization of value-chain participation in Vietnam, a regionalization that was common to nearly all sectors.

4.5 Linking the Evolution of GVCs to Contemporary Debates on GVCs and Development

This chapter has documented the level and positioning of Asian countries in GVCs. In doing so, it has highlighted the heterogeneous performance in GVCs and recent dynamics. While many countries have integrated substantially in

GVCs, few have integrated to an extent greater than would be expected by their size. More tellingly, a substantial number of countries have not been able to integrate adequately into value chains, particularly those in South and Central Asia.

Countries have also been shown to take very different positions in GVCs, with some focused upon assembly activities and others situated upstream. Even here, however, there are important differences, with some countries reliant upon the extraction and export of natural resources and others the production and export of parts and components. These different positionings in GVCs provide different opportunities for economic advancement and the building of the domestic capabilities needed for long-run growth and development. This also provides an important motivation for analysis and policy interventions to improve a country's positioning and diversification in GVCs.

The analysis further highlights relevant dynamics. One aspect of this is the shifting position of countries within GVCs, with many of them increasing integration levels and their share in global GVC activity. This has often involved the reinforcement of an existing specialization in either forward or backward linkages, with few countries showing increased integration along both linkages. Over the period considered, GVCs in Asia also seem to have become more regional, with the average distance of countries to their suppliers and buyers diminishing. These reasons may include the relatively high growth of Asia which has increased demand and created opportunities for firms in regional value chains. It could also be the consequence of a fragmenting global economy, driven by trade and geopolitical tensions that are limiting opportunities for GVC integration beyond Asia.

The dataset used ends in 2019. This has the advantage of avoiding the short-term turbulence caused by COVID-19, allowing for a more focused analysis on longer term trends. At the same time, this also means that some of the latest developments are not accounted for. While the disruption caused by COVID-19 was short-lived, with GVCs shown to be resilient to this major shock (World Trade Organization 2023, Chapter 2), the pandemic has potentially exacerbated existing tensions and set in motion developments that can have longer term impacts. Concerns around supply chain shortages and disruptions, particularly those due to long and complex supply chains, have led to increased calls for reshoring, nearshoring, and friendshoring, with the European Union, among others, calling for increased strategic autonomy. These ideas have been reflected in recent approaches to industrial policy, including the CHIPS Act and the Inflation Reduction Act in the USA. To the extent that these efforts are successful, there are potential consequences for the functioning of GVCs and the opportunities that developing countries have in integrating into and upgrading in, GVCs.

The examples of China and Vietnam also highlight the fact that developments in a country's GVC integration and positioning are not independent of developments in others. The reasons for the decline in China's GVC integration indicators are varied. This reflects a shift in the role of China in GVCs and efforts to increase the domestic value added in China's final output through its "Made in China 2025" policy and ongoing efforts to engage in high-quality development. It also reflects weakening competitiveness in China, driven partly by rising wages but also by geopolitical tensions that are raising the costs and the risks from producing in China.

These dynamics are creating opportunities for other countries, with Vietnam being a significant beneficiary. Investments into Vietnam by Western firms have increased dramatically in recent years, while that into China has subsided. This is partly the result of efforts to lessen the risk of foreign investment, with firms adopting a China+1 policy to their supply chain activity. Investment by Chinese firms in Vietnam has also risen rapidly in recent years. One rationale for this is to help avoid protectionist measures by the USA (and others) targeting China specifically, using Vietnam as an assembler and link to the USA, thus avoiding protectionist measures on direct trade between China and the USA.

Overall, the analysis and this discussion highlight the myriad factors driving a country's possibilities and integration into GVCs. Domestic resources and capabilities, along with economic policy, can influence the integration of countries into GVCs, but the very nature of GVCs means that external factors are also relevant. The strong interdependence of countries in GVCs means that geopolitics will be an important factor in driving the future dynamics of GVCs, while opportunities for individual countries will also depend on the changes in the economic performance and competitiveness of other countries in a process that could resemble a "flying geese" type model (Kojima 2000).

5 Economic Complexity in Global Value Chains in Asia

5.1 Introduction: Complexity and Development

Recent work has highlighted the importance of economic complexity for economic growth and development (Hausmann et al. 2014). Complexity is an attribute of both products and economies. The complexity of an exported (or imported) product captures the sophistication or uniqueness (measured by the number of countries that successfully export a product) of the capabilities that are needed to produce and sell it successfully in international markets. Relatedly, the complexity of an economy reflects the number and kinds of products that it can export successfully. The set of products exported successfully is an indicator of the capabilities that are present in the firms located in the economy. In short, more complex products are those that are exported by more complex economies, and more complex economies are those that can export more complex products.

The Innovation and Structural Transformation Database combines information on complexity – particularly the complexity of products – with information on global value chain (GVC) integration to define indicators on the complexity of the inputs that are part of the production process and the complexity of final output for a variety of sectors. Through these indicators, the database provides an overview of the quality or complexity of various contributions to value chains, dimensions that are not captured by more standard GVC indicators. In particular, the database provides information on the complexity of the intermediate products that are supplied to a sector within an economy for its final production. It further distinguishes between the complexity of foreign (imported) intermediates and domestically produced intermediates. It also provides information on the complexity of the final output that is produced by the sector of interest.

The database thus allows for a comparison between input and output complexity. This comparison is linked to the idea of upgrading within GVCs, with successful economies moving toward activities within value chains that offer opportunities for capturing a greater share of the value added and improving the quality and complexity of domestic production within value chains. Underlying this approach is the idea that sectors receive intermediates of a

DOI: 10.4324/9781003590330-5

certain complexity level for production, which are then translated into outputs. While it may be expected that the outputs will be more complex than the inputs, this is not necessarily the case, with the capabilities needed to assemble a final good potentially less demanding than those needed to produce the intermediate inputs. Successful sectors and economies could be considered to be those that are able to upgrade their output complexity or that are able to improve the complexity of their domestic inputs relative to that of foreign inputs.

This chapter uses the information in the Innovation and Structural Transformation Database (Foster-McGregor et al. 2024a, 2024b) to examine the relationship between the complexity of inputs into the production process and the complexity of the resulting output, with a focus on the complexity of foreign inputs. The chapter further examines whether there is a relationship between the complexity of both foreign inputs and output and GVC integration and analyzes whether deeper GVC integration may be considered to be either a driver of, or a consequence of, improvements in the complexity of production. To illustrate these relationships, the chapter focuses on two sectors that are often considered GVC sectors and that are examples of a relatively high-technology, electrical and optical, and low-technology sector, textiles. Specifically, the indicators used out of the full list provided in Chapter 1, Table A1, are as follows (file *DB_Input_And_Output_Complexities.xlsx*): Domestic Input Complexity; Foreign Input Complexity; Output Complexity; Overall Complexity.

5.2 Complexity as a Measure of Upgrading

The idea of product complexity was introduced by Hidalgo and Hausmann (2009) but has since undergone significant methodological changes. These authors started from the idea that a comparative advantage in exporting a specific product indicates the presence of specific production capabilities needed for the product. Then product ubiquity (how many countries export a product with comparative advantage) can be seen as a measure of how common the presence of the product-specific capabilities is. Diversity (how many products a country exports with comparative advantage) is a measure of the extent of a country's capabilities. In Hidalgo and Hausmann (2009), product complexity was derived from an iterative procedure called the "method of reflections," in which product ubiquity and country diversity were fed each other, such that the resulting diversity measure took account of the ubiquity of products, and the latter took account of country diversity. Felipe et al. (2012) offer an early application of this method.

Later on (e.g., Hausmann et al. 2014), the method to calculate product complexity evolved into a question of solving an eigenvalue problem. A summary of the technical details is provided in Box 5.1 (this is advanced material that can be skipped). In terms of capabilities, the implication is that the average product complexity (PCI) can be assumed to capture the production capabilities that are needed to produce products that highly developed countries produce. This

> **Box 5.1 Complexity, Eigenvalues, and Correspondence Analysis**
>
> The transformation of the original method of reflections into an eigenvalue problem makes it equivalent to what quantitative ecologists such as Legendre and Legendre (1998) call correspondence analysis (Mealy et al. 2019; Van Dam et al. 2021). In this procedure, the product-by-country matrix of binary comparative advantages is transformed and then used to derive eigenvalues and eigenvectors. Product complexity is the leading eigenvector of such a transformed matrix. The country-level economic complexity index (ECI) is calculated as the average product complexity (PCI) of the products in which the country has comparative advantage. Alternatively, we start with the country-by-product binary Revealed Comparative Advantage (RCA) matrix, and ECI is derived as the leading eigenvector, while PCI is the average ECI of the countries that have comparative advantage in the product. These two approaches are equivalent up to a multiplicative factor.
>
> Correspondence analysis is a descriptive method aimed at reducing the dimension of the analysis. This has implications for the interpretation of complexity. If we start with a large number of products (around 5,000 in the most detailed disaggregation level), we can look at our dataset as a 5,000-dimensional space in which countries are positioned by their comparative advantages. Correspondence analysis (i.e., the method of complexity) reduces this to a one-dimensional space (although > one-dimensional spaces are also possible by looking at further eigenvectors; see Nomaler and Verspagen 2024). The one-dimensional ECI turns out to be strongly correlated to GDP per capita (we will provide an example below), which allows the interpretation of ECI as an indicator of economic development.
>
> Source: Authors

is why we will use PCI as a way to operationalize the notion of upgrading. If a country acquires comparative advantage in a product with high PCI, it means that it acquired production capabilities that are associated with highly developed countries. This also represents a tendency for the ECI of the country to rise.

Figure 5.1 illustrates these characteristics of the ECI and PCI. On the left side of the figure, we plot (the log of) GDP per capita against the ECI. We use the dataset employed in Nomaler and Verspagen (2024), for the year 2018. We see a clear positive correlation between ECI and the development level as indicated by GDP per capita. On the right-hand side of the figure, we plot the so-called centroids (ubiquity-weighted averages) of the PCI in 11 different categories of the Lall classification scheme (Lall 2000). Although these centroids

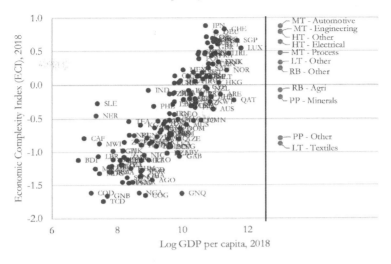

Figure 5.1 Complexity and Development
Source: Authors

do not have a value on the horizontal axis (GDP per capita), they do share the measurement scale of ECI on the vertical axis on the left (see Legendre and Legendre 1998; Nomaler and Verspagen 2024 for technical details).

Of the 11 Lall groups, the "PP – Other" (PP for primary products, while Other refers mostly to agricultural resources) and "LT – textiles" (LT for low-technology) are the groups with the lowest complexity values. "PP – minerals" and "RB- Agri" (RB for resource-based manufacturing, Agri for mostly agricultural resources) rank higher but still have negative values. The highest ranking groups in terms of complexity are medium-tech ("MT") Automotive and Engineering (e.g., machinery) products. The high-tech groups ("HT"), electrical and other, rank just below that.

The combination of ECI and PCI of the Lall groups on the vertical axis of Figure 5.1 represents the way we must interpret complexity. Complexity tells us how the comparative advantage of a product relates to development levels: products with high (low) complexity tend to be exported (with comparative advantage) by countries with high (low) development levels. This makes complexity a good basis to evaluate upgrading. When a country gains a comparative advantage in a high-complexity product, it moves into the direction of a specialization pattern that is typically associated with development.

The GVC complexity measures are based on the input-output accounting framework that is used to construct indicators for global value chains (Chapter 4). In order to relate product complexity to GVCs, we first assign detailed five-digit Harmonized System products to the sectors in the input-output tables, using a concordance by Eurostat. We also apply the Hausmann-Hidalgo

ECI algorithm to calculate product complexity for each year, and z-score the product complexity variable.[1] We use the BEC classification to distinguish intermediate goods and final goods at the five-digit level.[2] A summary is provided in Box 5.2, and the technical details are in Foster-McGregor et al. (2024b).

Box 5.2   The GVC-Complexity Measures

All GVC-complexity variables are calculated at the level of a country-sector combination, e.g., the textiles industry in Malaysia. Final Output Complexity of the country-sector is equal to the weighted average of complexity of all final products, where the weights are export value shares of the product in the country-sector's total final goods exports. We use the data from exports in Harmonized System products to calculate those weights. A similar procedure is used to calculate the average complexity of intermediate goods exported by the country-sector.

Based on the latter indicator (complexity of intermediate products), input-complexity of the GVC that corresponds to the country-sector can be defined. For this, we first "decompose" the value of final demand served by the chain (country-sector) into contributions of all country-sectors in the input-output table, using a standard input-output methodology that is also used in Chapter 4. This includes the country-sector of the GVC itself, but for this contribution, we subtract the value added corresponding to final demand served by the country-sector, so that only value from intermediate deliveries is counted.

We use these values to construct shares (of all country-sector combinations) of intermediate value deliveries to a specific country-sector. For example, we have the share of both the Japanese basic metals sector and the Chinese rubber sector in total intermediate value delivered to the Indian transport equipment sector. These shares are combined with the intermediate goods complexities of the delivering sector to create input complexity of the country-sector that takes the deliveries. In terms of the example, we use the complexity of intermediate goods delivered by the Chinese rubber sector and the Japanese basic metals sector in the calculation of input complexity of the Indian transport equipment sector. We distinguish between domestic and foreign sectors in the calculation of input complexity. Within these categories, the weights of the delivering sectors sum to one.

Source: Authors

5.3 Foreign and Domestic Input Complexity Are Complementary in the Production Process

Figures 5.2 and 5.3 provide information on the levels of domestic and foreign input complexity in 2007 for the electrical and optical equipment sector (Electricals) and textiles and textile products sector (Textiles). The figures provide insights into whether the complexity of foreign and domestic inputs into production are similar or whether economies rely on one source of inputs more than the other source in obtaining complex inputs. Overall, the figures reveal that there is a strong positive association between domestic and foreign input complexity levels in the two sectors, implying that economies with high domestic input complexity also tend to have high levels of foreign input complexity. This positive association is stronger in the case of textiles, while in the case of electricals, there are several economies that have relatively low levels of domestic input complexity and relatively high levels of foreign input complexity. This group includes Asian countries such as Lao PDR, Cambodia, Indonesia, and Pakistan, among others. For this group of economies, therefore, there is some evidence to suggest that they rely extensively on foreign intermediates for their complex inputs in electricals.

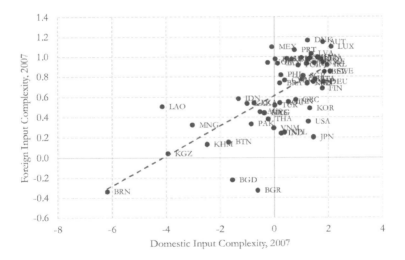

Figure 5.2 Comparison of 2007 Levels of Domestic and Foreign Input Complexity in Electricals

Note: Dotted line is the line of best fit.

Source: Authors based on information from the Innovation and Structural Transformation Database

68 *Innovation and Structural Transformation in Asia*

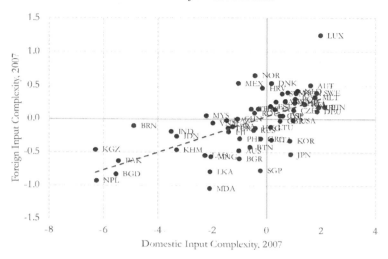

Figure 5.3 Comparison of 2007 Levels of Domestic and Foreign Input Complexity in Textiles

Note: Dotted line is the line of best fit.
Source: Authors based on information from the Innovation and Structural Transformation Database

5.4 The Production Activities of Asian Economies Often Rely on Relatively Low Complexity Foreign Inputs

Figures 5.4 and 5.5 report information on foreign input complexity in 2007 along with the change between 2007 and 2019 for electricals and textiles, respectively. The economies reporting the highest values of foreign input complexity in the case of electricals tend to be the more advanced European economies as well as economies such as Mexico, which is strongly integrated into US value chains. Asian economies appear in the middle and bottom of the distribution, signaling that they are either not engaged intensively in the production of electrical goods requiring complex intermediates or that the economies are able to produce complex intermediates themselves. Combined with the information in Figure 5.2, the data show that Cambodia, for example, is an economy not engaged in the production of goods requiring complex intermediates. This is because it has low domestic and foreign input complexity. Japan, at the other extreme, is an economy able to produce complex intermediates, as signified by the relatively high level of domestic input complexity and low level of foreign input complexity (in 2007). Considering changes over time, foreign input complexity has risen over time in many economies. Increases have been particularly pronounced in the Philippines, Vietnam, and Bangladesh. Such results may suggest an improvement in capabilities and the

Economic Complexity in Global Value Chains in Asia 69

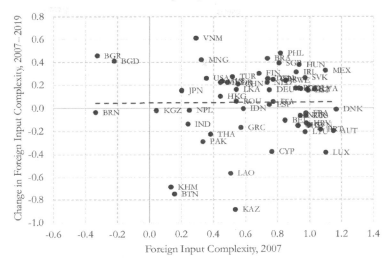

Figure 5.4 Foreign Input Complexity in 2007 and Change Between 2007 and 2019 in Electricals

Note: Dotted line is the line of best fit.

Source: Authors based on information from the Innovation and Structural Transformation Database

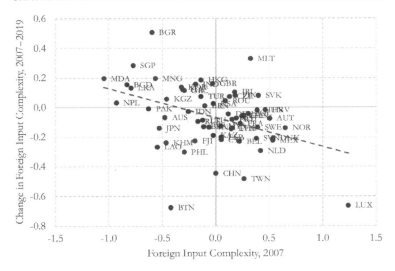

Figure 5.5 Foreign Input Complexity in 2007 and Change Between 2007 and 2019 in Textiles

Note: Dotted line is the line of best fit.

Source: Authors based on information from the Innovation and Structural Transformation Database

complexity of electricals production in these economies, with a movement toward the production of more sophisticated products requiring more sophisticated inputs. Conversely, foreign input complexity declined in Kazakhstan, Lao PDR, Bhutan, and Cambodia.

Figure 5.5 reports the ranking of countries in terms of initial foreign input complexity in textiles. It shows some similarities to that for electricals, with advanced economies in Europe and North America tending to report relatively high values of foreign input complexity and many Asian countries reporting relatively low values. There are exceptions to this general pattern, however, with Taiwan showing a relatively high initial value of foreign input complexity. Over time, there have been declines in foreign input complexity in textiles for many economies, albeit several economies with low initial levels of complexity saw relatively large increases. These include a few Asian countries such as Pakistan, Sri Lanka, Bangladesh, and Nepal, possibly reflecting their increasing integration into textiles global value chains.

5.5 The Complexity of Foreign and Domestic Intermediates of the Asian Economies Has Tended to Increase Over Time

The previous two figures highlight different dynamics of foreign input complexity. As mentioned, some of these dynamics may have different interpretations depending on developments in domestic input complexity. An increase in foreign input complexity, for example, could reflect an upgrading of production capabilities, but if combined with a decline in domestic input complexity may also suggest a downgrading of capabilities in the intermediates sector.

To shed further light on these dynamics, Figures 5.6 and 5.7 report scatterplots of the change in foreign and domestic input complexity for electricals and textiles, respectively. The figures can be split into four quadrants: (i) the upper-right quadrant contains cases where both domestic and foreign input complexity have increased; (ii) the upper-left quadrant, where foreign input complexity has risen and domestic input complexity has fallen; (iii) the lower-left quadrant, where both domestic and foreign input complexity has fallen; and (iv) the lower-right quadrant, where domestic input complexity has increased, but foreign input complexity has decreased. Quadrants (i) and (iv) contain cases of domestic upgrading in terms of intermediate production, quadrant (ii) a case of downgrading in terms of intermediate production (but not necessarily final production), and quadrant (iii) a case of intermediate downgrading (and likely a downgrading of final production capabilities).

Considering the case of electricals (Figure 5.6), many Asian economies have experienced an improvement in both foreign and domestic input complexity, including the Philippines, Singapore, South Korea, Japan, China, Mongolia, and Taiwan. Conversely, there is little evidence of input downgrading in the Asian economies. In other Asian countries, there is evidence of increasing domestic input complexity at the expense of foreign input complexity. This is the case

Economic Complexity in Global Value Chains in Asia   71

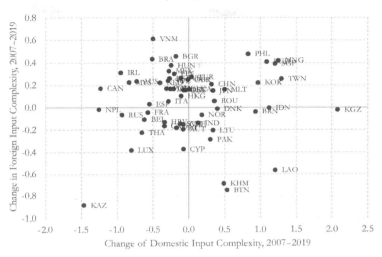

Figure 5.6 Change in Domestic and Foreign Input Complexity in Electricals, 2007–2019

Source: Authors based on information from the Innovation and Structural Transformation Database

for Bhutan, Cambodia, Pakistan, Indonesia, India, Kyrgyz Republic, and Lao PDR. Many advanced European economies appear in the upper-left quadrant, suggesting an improvement in foreign input complexity at the expense of domestic input complexity. This is also the case for Malaysia, Hong Kong, and

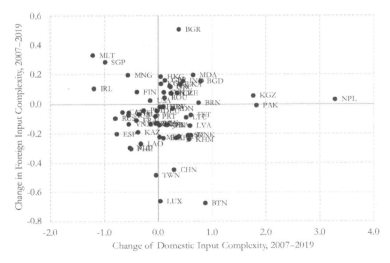

Figure 5.7 Change in Domestic and Foreign Input Complexity in Textiles, 2007–2019

Source: Authors based on information from the Innovation and Structural Transformation Database

particularly Vietnam. In this latter case, these developments may suggest an increasing role in assembly activities in electricals within GVCs, using complex intermediates from abroad in their assembly activities.

In the case of textiles (Figure 5.7), few economies have seen an increase in foreign input complexity at the expense of domestic input complexity. Mongolia and Singapore are two examples of such economies. There are a small number of economies that have experienced an improvement in domestic input complexity at the expense of foreign input complexity, e.g., Bhutan, Cambodia, and Pakistan. Such results imply that most economies have seen either increases or decreases along both dimensions, a result consistent with the strong positive relationship observed between domestic and foreign input complexity for textiles in Figure 5.3. Such an outcome suggests a strong complementary relationship between domestic and foreign input complexity and capabilities in the case of textiles.

5.6 The Asian Economies Have Been Able to Upgrade Final Output Complexity of Electricals and Textiles

We now analyze the complexity of GVCs. This is done by examining developments in the complexity of inputs used in the production process and the extent to which this complexity is provided by foreign or domestic sources. Of interest is whether backward integration into GVCs allows for upgrading of production activities, questioning whether improvements in the complexity of foreign intermediate inputs translate into improvements in the complexity of final output. To examine this, Figures 5.8 and 5.9 report information on the change in foreign input complexity and the change in domestic final output complexity for electricals and textiles, respectively.

In the case of electricals (Figure 5.8), most economies have seen an increase in foreign input complexity over time, with the majority of these also seeing an increase in final output complexity. As such, there is evidence that final output complexity rises with foreign input complexity for many countries, including Asian countries such as Japan, Vietnam, and the Philippines. The case of Vietnam is an interesting one, with rising foreign input complexity and final output complexity, combined with declining domestic input complexity. Such results are consistent with the view expressed above regarding increased GVC integration. Indeed, Vietnam has moved to the production of more complex final electrical goods, relying on more complex foreign intermediates to achieve this. While there are a few cases where rising foreign input complexity is associated with declining final output complexity, the declines in final output complexity tend to be relatively small. This leaves two further sets of economies. The first group – including Pakistan, India, and Cambodia – has witnessed declines in both foreign input complexity and final output complexity over time, suggesting a downgrading of final output production. The second group – including Lao PDR, Bhutan, Brunei Darussalam, Nepal, and Taiwan – has combined rising final output complexity with lower foreign input complexity. This group also

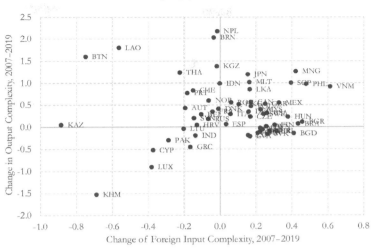

Figure 5.8 Changes in Foreign Input Complexity Versus Changes in Final Output Complexity in Electricals, 2007–2019

Source: Authors based on information from the Innovation and Structural Transformation Database

represents examples of upgrading of final production, therefore, but in this case not by using complex foreign intermediates in GVCs.

In the case of textiles (Figure 5.9), examples of upgrading in both foreign input complexity and final output complexity are Singapore,

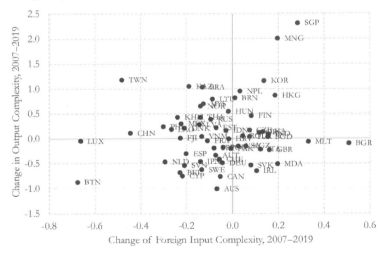

Figure 5.9 Changes in Foreign Input Complexity Versus Changes in Final Output Complexity in Textiles, 2007–2019

Source: Authors based on information from the Innovation and Structural Transformation Database

Mongolia, South Korea, Hong Kong, India, Bangladesh, Nepal, and Brunei Darussalam. As such, the results suggest an important role for GVCs in upgrading within the textiles sector in these economies. In comparison to electricals, there are more examples of falling final output complexity alongside rising foreign input complexity, though these examples tend not to be Asian economies. A number of economies are found to downgrade along both dimensions. Examples are Japan, Vietnam, and Bhutan. Finally, many economies saw increases in final output complexity alongside declines in foreign input complexity. These include China, Taiwan, Kazakhstan, Cambodia, the Philippines, Lao PDR, Thailand, and Indonesia. In these cases, the evidence suggests that final output upgrading has occurred without the use of complex foreign intermediate inputs available through GVCs, suggesting a reliance on domestic intermediate capabilities in improving final output complexity.

5.7 Increased GVC Integration Does Not Necessarily Require or Imply Increased Input Complexity Through Foreign Intermediate Inputs

As highlighted above, it is useful to think of developments in input and output complexity as being strongly related to GVCs as a development strategy. In this section, data from the Innovation and Structural Transformation Database on GVC integration are combined with the complexity data to address whether deeper integration into GVCs is associated with receiving more complexity through foreign intermediates in the two sectors of interest. In particular, information on the change in the share of foreign value added in total final demand served by the sector – an indicator of backward integration in GVCs – is compared with information on changes in the degree of foreign input complexity. Results for the electricals and textiles sectors are reported in Figures 5.9 and 5.10, respectively.

Results for electricals (Figure 5.10) suggest that there is not a strong relationship between changes in backward integration in GVCs (as captured by the change in the foreign share of value added) and the change in foreign complexity. Many economies have seen higher levels of backward GVC integration and at the same time reductions in foreign input complexity (lower right quadrant), perhaps suggesting a movement toward more complex own production in GVCs. At the same time, there are also many economies that have experienced higher levels of backward GVC participation alongside an increase in foreign input complexity (upper right quadrant). While there are relatively few economies that have seen a decline in both backward GVC participation and foreign input complexity, many have seen lower levels of backward integration alongside increases in foreign input complexity, which may be interpreted as downgrading – i.e., economies that have become more reliant upon foreign complexity, corresponding with an overall reduction in backward integration.

The case of textiles (Figure 5.11) results in a similar story, with many economies seeing an increase in backward GVC participation over time, but

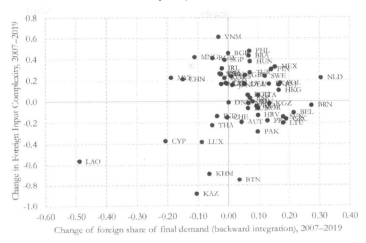

Figure 5.10 Change in Foreign Value-Added Share Versus Change in Foreign Input Complexity in Electricals, 2007–2019

Source: Authors based on information from the Innovation and Structural Transformation Database

they roughly equally spread between economies that have also seen an increase in foreign input complexity and those that have seen a decline. While few economies have seen a decline across both dimensions, there are again many economies that have seen increased foreign input complexity alongside

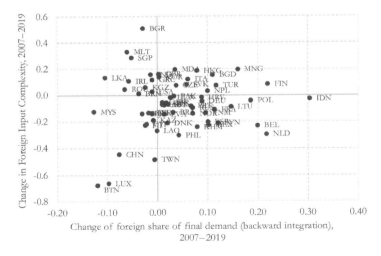

Figure 5.11 Change in Foreign Value-Added Share Versus Change in Foreign Input Complexity in Textiles, 2007–2019

Source: Authors based on information from the Innovation and Structural Transformation Database

declining GVC integration. The Asian economies appear in all four quadrants of Figure 5.11, accounting for a large share of the total number of economies that have seen declining GVC participation alongside rising foreign input complexity – this group includes South Korea, Hong Kong, Bangladesh, Nepal, and Mongolia.

5.8 Increased Backward GVC Integration Is Not Necessarily a Requirement or Response to Improved Final Output Complexity

This final section completes the analysis of the link between backward GVC integration and the complexity of production by asking whether there is a relationship between increased GVC integration and the complexity of final production. Such a positive association would suggest that success in integrating into GVCs goes hand in hand with improvements in the complexity of final goods produced within GVCs. Results are reported in Figures 5.12 and 5.13 for electricals and textiles, respectively.

Similar to the case of foreign input complexity, results for electricals (Figure 5.12) suggest no strong relationship between GVC integration and final output complexity. A fairly large group of Asian countries showed signs of improving both GVC integration and final output complexity: Brunei Darussalam, Nepal, Bhutan, Hong Kong, Kyrgyz Republic, South Korea,

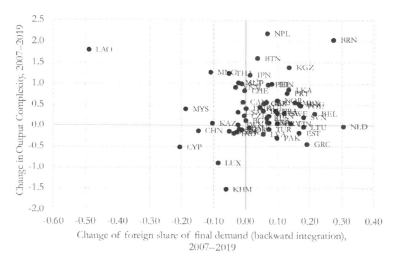

Figure 5.12 Change in Foreign Value-Added Share Versus Change in Final Output Complexity in Electricals, 2007–2019

Source: Authors based on information from the Innovation and Structural Transformation Database

Economic Complexity in Global Value Chains in Asia 77

Japan, the Philippines, and Sri Lanka. Some economies – including Pakistan – were able to further integrate into GVCs while seeing a reduction in final output complexity, suggesting a potential downgrading of final production in electricals GVCs. There are also several Asian economies that have seen lower levels of backward GVC integration alongside rising final output complexity. These include Lao PDR, Malaysia, Mongolia, Thailand, Vietnam, and Kazakhstan. These economies represent cases of upgrading in the sense that they have been able to increase the complexity of their final output, while having a lower share of foreign value added in total value added. As such, they are not only improving the complexity of their final output, but also doing this in the context of capturing a greater share of the value added from production (as indicated by the falling share of foreign value added in total value added).

In the case of textiles (Figure 5.13), a majority of economies have seen an increase in backward GVC integration in textiles over time, with slightly more of those also seeing an increase in final output complexity than those witnessing a decline. While the Asian economies appear in all four quadrants, they again make up a relatively high share of the economies that have seen declining GVC integration alongside rising final output complexity – examples being China, Malaysia, Thailand, Brunei Darussalam, and Lao PDR.

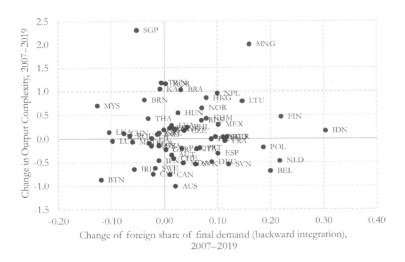

Figure 5.13 Change in Foreign Value-Added Share Versus Change in Final Output Complexity in Textiles, 2007–2019

Source: Authors based on information from the Innovation and Structural Transformation Database

Notes

1 z-Score is a statistical measurement that describes a value's relationship to the mean of a group of values. z-Score is measured in terms of standard deviations from the mean.
2 BEC stands for Broad Economic Categories: https://unstats.un.org/unsd/trade/classifications/bec.asp.

6 The Fourth Industrial Revolution Technologies in Asia

6.1 Introduction: Innovation in Fourth Industrial Revolution Technologies Is Changing the Way We Live, Work, and Interact

The Fourth Industrial Revolution (4IR) refers to an ongoing and rapid technological revolution associated with digital and other related technologies. This revolution involves a move away from *analog*, mechanical and electronic technology toward *digital* technology. With analog technologies, one does not read time, weight, sound, etc., directly. Take an analog watch. The hands' movements over the dial are a way of representing passing time. It is not the same thing as time itself: it is a representation or an analogy of time.

The term "digital," applies to any technological device that functions through a binary computational code, such as mobile phones, tablets, laptops, computers, etc. It refers to how information is stored and transmitted. When it is done in digital format, it is converted into numbers – at the most basic machine level as "zeroes and ones." The term represents technology that relies on the use of microprocessors; hence, computers and applications that are dependent on computers such as the Internet, as well as other devices such as video cameras, and mobile devices such as phones and personal-digital assistants (PDAs). A digital watch displays time by automatically showing readings on an LCD display instead of using analog pointers and dials.

The use of digital technologies has had a big impact on four areas: computing, energy, biology, and manufacturing. The new and emerging technologies associated with the 4IR are widely considered to be shaping a new landscape in the way we live, work, and interact. These technologies include robotics, additive manufacturing, artificial intelligence, the internet of things, and big data. A key feature of these technologies is the growing interconnection and complementarity between digital, physical, and biological production systems. While many of these technologies are not new, what is new is their interconnection or fusion, which is much higher than during previous industrial revolutions. They are to some extent in their infancy in terms of the General-Purpose Technologies that will emerge out of them. Yet, the speed

DOI: 10.4324/9781003590330-6

of the development of these technologies and the potential for their use has raised enormous expectations about the potential of the 4IR.

Given the scale, scope, and complexity of the developments that this digital revolution may entail, there is a strong expectation that the 4IR will fundamentally alter the way we live, the way we work, and the way we communicate and interact with each other. Many of these changes are likely to be positive, improving productivity, raising global income levels, improving the quality of life for populations around the world, and potentially helping solve other global challenges such as climate change. At the same time, there is a further expectation of negative impacts of the 4IR. One particular concern relates to the impact of these new technologies on the world of work. Indeed, there is fear that some new digital technologies may substitute for a wide array of activities and tasks currently undertaken by workers, which may lead to widespread technological unemployment (Acemoglu and Restrepo 2019). That such technologies are more likely to substitute for more middle-skilled and routine jobs may also lead to a more strongly segregated labor market, with the co-existence of a low-skill and low-pay segment and a high-skill and high-pay segment, which in turn could impact the levels of inequality within economies (Das and Hilgenstock 2022).

This chapter uses data from the Innovation and Structural Transformation Database (Foster-McGregor et al. 2024a, 2024b) to examine the involvement of Asian countries in 4IR technologies. The analysis focuses on three dimensions of engagement in the 4IR, over the period 2007–2019: the development of 4IR technologies through innovation resulting in patents, the production and export of 4IR technologies, and the import and use of 4IR technologies. The evidence from previous industrial revolutions suggests that the largest beneficiaries from the revolutions are the innovators and the providers of the key intellectual capital on which the revolution is founded. As we shall see, it remains the case that 4IR innovations are highly concentrated within a small number of developed economies. For most economies, therefore, the benefits from 4IR technologies are likely to come from other sources. One source relates to the production of capital goods that embody 4IR technologies. With the fragmentation of production associated with global value chains having increased in recent decades, there is a possibility that some developing economies can enter into the production of 4IR-based technologies without having undertaken the innovation themselves. One proxy for the extent of such engagement is the value of exports of 4IR products. A second proxy would be imports of 4IR technologies.

Specifically, the indicators used out of the full list provided in Chapter 1, Table A1, are as follows: (i) file *DB_Structural_Change_Basic_Indicators.xlsx*: RCA_CADCAM; RCA_ICT; RCA_RegInstr; RCA_Robots; RCA_Welding; RCA_3D; RCA_4IR; CADCAM_4IRsh; RegInstr_4IRsh; Robots_4IRsh; Welding_4IRsh; 3D_4IRsh; RCA_4IR_CADCAM; RCA_4IR_ICT; RCA_4IR_RegInstr; RCA_4IR_Robots; RCA_4IR_Welding; RCA_4IR_3D; (ii) file *DB_IR4patents_2000_2019.xlsx*: Nr Families; Nr. Families 10 Year Cumulative; Nr Families 10 Year All Technologies.

6.2 Patenting in 4IR Technologies

The notion of a Fourth Industrial Revolution is not a well-defined statistical concept. Different analysts and researchers have defined the concept in different ways, and some have not defined it in a strict sense at all. Most contributors to the debate agree that new digital components are an important part of the 4IR, but these are applied to a range of other technological fields, e.g., combinatorial chemistry. Within the category of digital technologies, automation and artificial intelligence are important concepts. Box 6.1 explains the type of information we use on patents, exports, and imports.

Figure 6.1 reports information on whether an economy had a Revealed Technological Advantage (RTA) in 4IR technologies in 2007 and 2019. The RTA is similar to the concept of Revealed Comparative Advantage (RCA) in the trade literature and essentially shows whether an economy is a more intensive producer of 4IR patents (relative to total patenting) than the world as a whole. The RTA indicator has been standardized in such a way that it lies

---

Box 6.1   Identifying 4IR Patents and Products

In order to collect statistics on the generation and use of 4IR technologies and products, we used data on patents and exports/imports. For the identification of patents that relate to 4IR technologies, we relied on a report by the European Patent Office (EPO 2020). In the appendix of this report, EPO provides a number of keywords and technology classes (IPC and CPC) that define a set of 4IR technologies and subfields thereof. We used this information to construct our own 4IR patent dataset. The EPO did not publish the raw data resulting from their analysis, but from summary statistics, we can see that our dataset is different from that one. This is due to the fact the EPO report does not document exactly how keywords and technology classes were combined, and also not how keywords were used exactly (e.g., full-text versus only titles and abstracts). Our own methodology and the resulting data are documented exactly in Menéndez et al. (2023).

For traded products, we relied on the UN's COMTRADE database, which contains data on imports and exports in the so-called Harmonized System that is used by customs services worldwide. We combined products that were identified in Foster-McGregor et al. (2019) and Acemoglu and Restrepo (2018). Further details of the trade data 4IR classification are available in Foster-McGregor et al. (2024b).

Source: Authors

82 Innovation and Structural Transformation in Asia

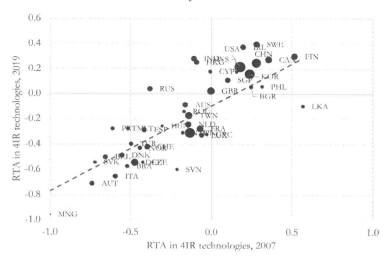

Figure 6.1 Revealed Technological Advantage in 4IR Technologies in 2007 and 2019
Source: Authors based on information from the Innovation and Structural Transformation Database

between −1 and 1, with positive (negative) values indicating that an economy is (not) specialized in 4IR technologies. The size of the dots in Figure 6.1 indicates the number of 4IR patent families[1] originating from the country. To construct the RTA used in Figure 6.1, data on the 10-year cumulative patenting in technologies are used.

The figure reveals that many Asian economies had positive RTA in 4IR technologies in 2007 and maintained that in 2019. This holds for Vietnam, the Philippines, China, Malaysia, and Singapore. Between 2007 and 2019, both Hong Kong and India developed an RTA in these technologies, while Sri Lanka lost RTA. Some of these results may appear somewhat surprising. The finding that Sri Lanka, the Philippines, and Vietnam had a positive index of RTA in 4IR technologies as far back as 2007 is somewhat unexpected. One reason for this is the definition of RTA, which does not take into account the absolute number of patents, but only involves a comparison of 4IR patenting with overall patenting in the country. An economy may have a high intensity of 4IR patenting despite having a small number of 4IR patents, with these patents accounting for a relatively high share of overall patents. This can help explain the results observed in Figure 6.1.

This can be seen from the size of dots in Figure 6.1, which indicate a very uneven size distribution of countries in terms of 4IR patenting in 2019. Figure 6.2 gives further details of this distribution by plotting the number of 4IR patent families in 2007 and 2019 against each other. The figure has a log scale, which compresses size differences between countries. At the top of the ranking, only eight economies had more than 1,000 patent families in the 4IR

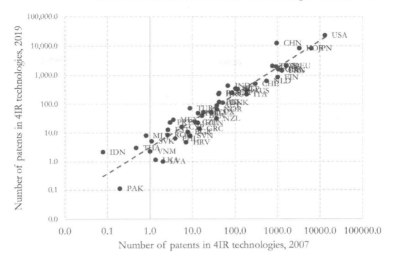

Figure 6.2 Number of 4IR Patent Families in 2007 and 2019

Note: Dotted line is the line of best fit.

Source: Authors based on information from the Innovation and Structural Transformation Database

in 2007, and this number increased to ten countries in 2019. Among those ten countries, four are Asian: Japan, South Korea, China, and Taiwan. Singapore and Hong Kong had more than 200 patent families in the 4IR in 2019, but all other Asian economies had less than 50 patent families in the 4IR in both 2007 and 2019. Thus, the positive RTA in 4IR technologies in a fair deal of Asian economies in Figure 6.1 was built on a relatively small number of patents, while other Asian countries appear as global technology leaders in the 4IR.

Considering changes over time, a large increase in 4IR patenting is observed in China, such that by 2019 it became the dominant economy in Asia for 4IR patenting, second in the world only to the USA. 4IR patenting also increased rapidly in South Korea and Taiwan. Despite a significant increase in the number of 4IR patents in Japan, it lost its second global position, dropping to fourth behind the USA, China, and Korea.

6.3 Trade in 4IR Products

Even if a country is not heavily engaged in patenting activities in 4IR technologies, it may still benefit from 4IR technologies either through the production of (capital) goods that embody 4IR technology or by using 4IR technologies in their production process. To capture these two dimensions, the Innovation and Structural Transformation Database reports information on the export and import of a set of products related to specific 4IR technologies, including CAD-CAM, 3D printing, Robots, Regulating instruments, ICT, and Automated welding machines.

Combining information on these different 4IR product categories, Figure 6.3 reports information on the value of the index of RCA in the export of 4IR products in 2007 and the change in the value of RCA between 2007 and 2019.[2] We document only Asian economies plus the USA and Germany as reference countries. Before discussing the results, it is worth highlighting that the RCA suffers from a problem similar to that of the RTA: an economy may have a high value of the RCA, despite having very low exports in 4IR products. This would be the case if the economy had low export values more generally, but where 4IR exports made up a relatively large share of these exports.

Turning to the results, it can be seen that nine economies had RCA greater than zero in the export of 4IR products in 2007 and 2019. These include the top four Asian economies in terms of 4IR patenting RTA: Japan, South Korea, China, and Taiwan. Other economies that had RTA greater than zero in the patenting of 4IR technologies (Malaysia, the Philippines, Singapore) also show up with positive RCA in Figure 6.3. Over time, a decline in the value of RCA is observed for most economies that had an RCA greater than zero in 2007 (the exceptions being the Philippines and Taiwan), though these economies tend to maintain their RCA greater than zero. Relatively large increases in RCA are observed in the cases of Vietnam and Lao PDR, with the RCA increasing above zero in the case of Vietnam. Overall, such results suggest that a handful of Asian countries have been able to engage in the production

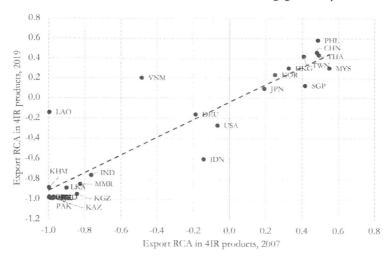

Figure 6.3 RCA in the Export of 4IR Products in 2007 and 2019

Note: Dotted line is the line of best fit.

Source: Authors based on information from the Innovation and Structural Transformation Database

and export of products embodying 4IR technologies. Most of these economies also perform relatively well in terms of patenting in 4IR technologies, suggesting a complementarity between the innovation activities and the production of goods embodying the resulting 4IR technology. There are exceptions to this, however, with Thailand and more recently Vietnam providing two examples of economies that are successful exporters of 4IR products despite a lack of RTA greater than zero in innovation in these technological areas.

A similar exercise can be undertaken on the import side. In this case, the question addressed is whether economies are intensive importers of 4IR products, which may suggest that they are users of 4IR technologies (irrespective of whether they are able to produce and export the products themselves). Results for 2007 and 2019 are presented in Figure 6.4.

Results for imports are largely similar to those for exports, with eight Asian economies (Hong Kong, Malaysia, the Philippines, Thailand, Singapore, China, South Korea, and Japan) and the USA having an RCA greater than zero on the import side in 2007 and 2019, all of which except the USA also had an RCA greater than zero on the export side. Taiwan is the only Asian country with an RTA larger than zero (in both 2007 and 2019) but RCA in imports lower than zero in 2007. In contrast to the export dimension, results for imports do suggest that more economies achieved RCA greater than zero between 2007 and 2019. Economies that gained an RCA in imports include India, Taiwan, and Vietnam, with Brunei Darussalam and Lao PDR also achieving large gains (albeit from low initial levels).

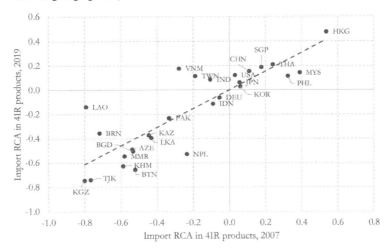

Figure 6.4 RCA in the Import of 4IR Products in 2007 and 2019

Note: Dotted line is the line of best fit.

Source: Authors based on information from the Innovation and Structural Transformation Database

6.4 Comparison in 4IR Production and Use in China and Japan

The analysis above suggests that a small number of Asian economies can be considered to innovate in 4IR technologies. Moreover, a similar set of economies tend to be the ones that have a specialization in both the import and export of 4IR technologies. As such, the results from the above analysis suggest a strong concentration in 4IR production and use, with most Asian economies currently largely excluded from the 4IR on both the production and use side.

This last section examines the performance of two economies in 2019: China and Japan. While both economies had an RCA greater than one in both the export and import of 4IR products, China had a strong RTA in 4IR patenting, while Japan did not have RTA greater than zero, despite having the highest number of 4IR patent families in 2019. This section compares the performance in the two economies by looking at the relative importance of technology subfields and the specific 4IR products in these two economies.

Figures 6.5 and 6.6 report information on the structure of patenting in China and Japan in 2019, respectively, with the cumulative number of patent families split into 19 technological subfields.[3] The two figures show a lot of similarities, with connectivity, home, and consumer goods accounting for a large share of all 4IR patents in both economies. At the same time, there are some noticeable differences. In particular, while these three

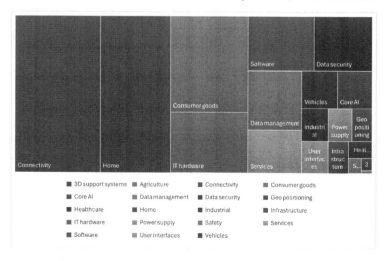

Figure 6.5 Tree Map of Cumulative Ten-Year Patent Families in China, 2019

Source: Authors based on information from the Innovation and Structural Transformation Database

The Fourth Industrial Revolution Technologies in Asia 87

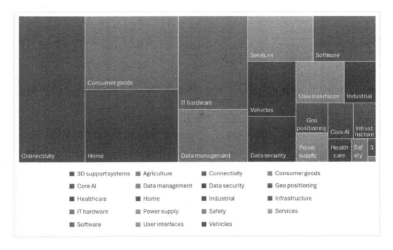

Figure 6.6 Tree Map of Cumulative Ten-Year Patent Families in Japan, 2019

Source: Authors based on information from the Innovation and Structural Transformation Database

subfields account for 57% of overall 4IR patenting in China, they account for just 45% in Japan, suggesting that Japan has a more diversified 4IR patent portfolio.

Figure 6.7 reports information on whether the two economies have an RTA greater than zero in each of the 19 technological subfields. Different from the results for overall 4IR patenting, this figure is constructed by looking at the importance of patenting in each of the technological subfields relative to total 4IR patenting, meaning that each economy will have RTA greater than one in at least a subset of technological fields.[4] The figure reveals that China has RTA greater than one in just two subfields, connectivity and home, while Japan has RTA greater than one in a wider range of subfields, including data management, IT hardware, industrial, safety, user interfaces, and vehicles.

The final two figures report information on RCA in 2019 for China and Japan in the different 4IR products in the case of exports and imports, respectively. In the case of exports (Figure 6.8), it can be seen that while China has RCA greater than zero in the case of ICT only, Japan has RCA greater than zero in all 4IR technologies except ICT, with particularly high RCAs in CAD-CAM, robots, and automated welding equipment. Such results align with the results for patenting, which further showed that Japan has a more diversified structure in terms of patenting. Conversely, in the case of imports (Figure 6.9), Japan is found to have RCA greater than one only in ICT, perhaps highlighting the fact that Japan is not an intensive exporter of such technologies. China is also found to have an import RCA in only one product category, robots.

88 *Innovation and Structural Transformation in Asia*

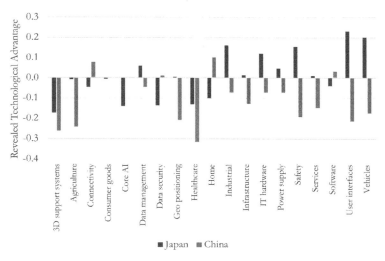

Figure 6.7 Revealed Technological Advantage in 4IR Subfields in China and Japan in 2019

Source: Authors based on information from the Innovation and Structural Transformation Database

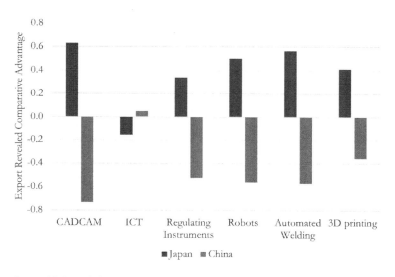

Figure 6.8 Revealed Comparative Advantage in the Export of 4IR Products in 2019

Source: Authors based on information from the Innovation and Structural Transformation Database

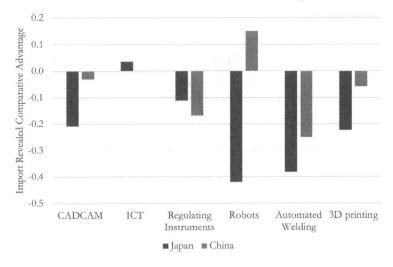

Figure 6.9 Revealed Comparative Advantage in the Import of 4IR Products in 2019
Source: Authors based on information from the Innovation and Structural Transformation Database

Overall, the results from this section highlight that even among the successful economies in the 4IR, there are different ways to integrate and different specialization patterns. The presence of RTA in subfields such as vehicles and export RCA in CAD-CAM and robots in Japan may suggest that there are certain path dependencies that encourage the development of 4IR subfields that link to historically important sectors and earlier technology vintages in economies.

Notes

1 A patent family refers to a set of patents taken out in different jurisdictions (e.g., different economies) on essentially the same invention. The use of a patent family rather than individual patents avoids double counting specific inventions. In the analysis, a patent family is considered to belong to the economy in which the inventor resides.
2 Revealed Comparative Advantage is constructed in a similar manner to the RTA as the share of 4IR exports in total exports relative to the share of 4IR exports in total global exports. As in the case of RTA, we rescale so that RCA lies between −1 and 1. A positive value is interpreted as the country having an RCA in the export of 4IR products (i.e., its export intensity in 4IR products is greater than that of the world as a whole).
3 The titles that are (partially) hidden in the figure for China are "Industrial," "User interfaces," "Geo Positioning," "Infrastructure," "Safety," "3D support systems," and "Agriculture" (in order of size). For Japan, the additional hidden title is "Healthcare."
4 Note that a patent family can appear in more than one technological subfield, meaning that the number of 4IR patents may be lower than the sum of the total patent families across all subfields.

7 Conclusions
Moderate Optimism About Asia's Development Prospects

This book has used the information in the Innovation and Structural Transformation Database created by the authors to assess development (https://dataverse.nl/dataverse/innovation_and_structural_transformation_database/) (Foster-McGregor et al. 2024a, 2024b). This database provides a wealth of information about productivity and structural transformation, global value chains (GVCs), complexity, and the Fourth Industrial Revolution (4IR). It has used this information to discuss Asia's development. The analysis departs from standard neoclassical discussions of factor accumulation and total factor productivity growth and is closer in spirit to heterodox analyses of structural transformation and capabilities (Chapter 2). Chapters 3 through 6 are written as essays using the indicators in the database. This final chapter provides some conclusions and final comments.

7.1 Chapter 3: Enhancing Labor Productivity Within Sectors Is Needed for Rapid Economic Growth

Improvements in living standards are, to a large extent, driven by improvements in productivity. The productivity performance of Asian countries over the last two decades has been highly heterogeneous, with some economies witnessing rapid annual growth rates of productivity, and others registering barely any productivity growth. In most economies, the major driver of aggregate productivity developments has been within-sector changes in productivity, with improvements in technology and increased capital utilization likely the major drivers of such productivity developments. Conversely, structural change has played a relatively minor role in the overall productivity performance of most economies.

Such conclusions are reflected in the results for two economies, China and Vietnam. China's productivity performance over the last two decades has been significantly stronger than Vietnam's, with developments within sectors being the major driver of such differences. Despite this, structural change has played a role in the relative performance of these two economies. In the case of Vietnam, there has been a strong shift out of agriculture, which has

DOI: 10.4324/9781003590330-7

contributed to overall productivity growth through a static structural change effect. Conversely, structural change in China has been less prominent, which has limited the role of this component in overall productivity growth. The shift to more dynamic sectors in the case of China has been more prominent than in Vietnam, however.

7.2 Chapter 4: Global Value Chains

Recently, concerns around the stagnation in GVC integration have been raised, with some suggesting the world is entering an era of "slowbalization." Developments in GVC integration of the Asian economies suggests a more nuanced conclusion, with a great deal of heterogeneity observed across the region. While there are many examples of economies that appear to have withdrawn from GVCs somewhat, others have increased their integration either by enhancing their forward or backward GVC integration or by increasing integration across both dimensions.

A more consistent picture emerges when considering the geographical dynamics of GVC integration, with the majority of the Asian economies seeing a decline in the average distance to GVC partners – through both backward and forward linkages. These developments suggest a move toward the increased regionalization of value chains in the region. Given recent developments and recent concerns about nearshoring and supply chain disruptions, it could be expected that this trend will continue in future years, a conclusion shared by Zhan et al. (2020).

China and Vietnam provide examples of the two extremes, namely decreasing and increasing GVC integration along both the backward and forward integration dimensions. China has become less integrated in GVCs in the recent period, while Vietnam has integrated further. Backward integration (e.g., assembly activities) continues to dominate Vietnam's GVC integration across a broad range of sectors, which may not present the greatest benefits from GVCs. Despite this, Vietnam has been able to move into more sophisticated value chains, also in terms of forward integration, with electrical and optical equipment perhaps providing the best example. Moreover, the integration of Vietnam has been driven by regional rather than global integration into value chains, a result different from that of China. Given recent developments and recent concerns about nearshoring and supply chain disruptions, a conclusion that could be drawn is that this may provide a more resilient way of integrating into value chains. Conversely, it could be argued that Vietnam has been able to replace the activities of China in many value chains in response to both the effect of increased protectionism (e.g., the US-China trade war) and to the deliberate efforts of China to rely more on the domestic market through its Made in China 2025 strategic plan.

7.3 Chapter 5: An Ambiguous Relationship Between Input and Output Complexity and GVC Integration

This chapter examined the inter-relationships between the complexity of inputs an economy uses in its production and both the complexity of the final output that the economy produces and the extent of backward integration into GVCs. To do this, it has focused on two sectors considered amenable to GVC-production, that is, to produce different parts of the product in different countries. They are examples of relatively high-technology (e.g., electrical) and low-technology sectors (e.g., textiles). Focusing on the complexity of inputs used in production, the analysis suggests that there is a positive association between domestic and foreign input complexity, indicating that they are, to some extent, complementary. This is particularly the case in textiles. Asian countries, however, are often found to have a relatively low level of complexity of foreign inputs – in both sectors – though they have often seen relatively large increases over time. Asian countries have also been able to upgrade the complexity of their final output over time, though this improvement is not always strongly related to the use of more complex foreign intermediates. In the case of electricals, improvements in final output complexity are often found to occur in combination with improvements in foreign input complexity – suggesting an important role for foreign inputs in upgrading opportunities in final production for these economies in electricals – but in the case of textiles, the improvement in final output complexity is often found to occur despite a decline in foreign input complexity – suggesting an important role for domestic input complexity in driving final output complexity. Despite these observed relationships between input and output complexity, the results suggest that there is little association between the extent of complexity upgrading – on both the input and output side – and developments in GVC integration. Deeper integration into GVCs can be accompanied by increases or decreases in foreign input complexity and increases or decreases in final output complexity. Such a result is perhaps not surprising – the major benefit of GVCs is argued to be that economies can find their niche in terms of sectors, activities and the complexity of production. The results do suggest, however, that GVC integration does not guarantee upgrading and that upgrading does not guarantee improved GVC performance.

7.4 Chapter 6: Divergent Performance in Fourth Industrial Revolution Innovation Across Asian Economies

The 4IR offers great hope for economic growth and increases in living standards but also presents various risks, the most prominent of which relates to the future of work. Historically, those economies that have benefitted the most from technological revolutions have been those that were engaged in the innovative activity that drives such revolutions. This chapter has used data from the Innovation and Structural Transformation Database to examine the extent to which Asian countries are involved in this kind of innovation and in the production of 4IR knowledge, as well as to examine the importance of imports and exports of 4IR products.

Results indicate that a small number of Asian countries contribute significantly to 4IR technology – notably Japan, China, and South Korea – while the majority of them are not involved in the production of 4IR technologies, leaving them at risk of being left behind and missing out on some of the benefits of the 4IR.

This weak performance of many regional members likely reflects more structural problems that result in a relatively poor performance in terms of innovation more generally. With a lack of capabilities in innovation unlikely to be solved in the short run, these economies will need to rely on the diffusion of such technologies, with two paths open to benefit from the 4IR. The first involves a movement into the production (and export) of goods that embody 4IR technologies, with an important role for inward FDI and globalization in developing capabilities and specialization in such production. The second involves the use of such goods embodying 4IR technologies in their production and the importation of such goods for consumption purposes. In both cases, these economies will be reliant upon the technological advances that are made in other economies. Considering the import and export of 4IR products, however, it is again found that a small number of Asian countries have comparative advantage in both the import and export of 4IR products, with these economies tending to be very similar to those with a comparative advantage in 4IR innovation. Such a conclusion raises the concern that economies that are not engaged in the production of 4IR technologies may miss out on some of the major gains from the 4IR, perpetuating existing income disparities and further exacerbating cross-economy inequality.

7.5 Final Comments About Asia's Future

The analysis of Asia based on the indicators in the Innovation and Structural Transformation Database indicates that the region can be divided into three groups of economies. First, the successful East Asian economies: China, Hong Kong, Japan, Singapore, South Korea, and Taiwan. These economies are high income (except China, middle income), and all of them have completed the traditional structural transformation process (the share of employment in agriculture is very low, except in China), have complex economies, participate in global value chains, and generate technologies of what is known as the Fourth Industrial Revolution. They will continue progressing. Further development of China poses questions that are not addressed in this book.

Second, a group of countries that have experienced structural transformation have become more complex and are integrated into global value chains (e.g., Malaysia, Thailand). Yet, these economies do not have the technological level of the first group and consequently are not key players in the generation of 4IR technologies. If they want to make it into the first group, they will have to invest significantly in R&D and create firms with advanced capabilities to produce capital goods and complex products in general.

Finally, the rest of Asia (most of it) trails far behind in most indicators: they still have large shares of workers in agriculture, they are not key players in global value chains, their economies are less complex than those of the previous two groups, and they do not generate advanced technologies. For this last group, we think development in the 21st century will be an uphill battle with slow progress. Some of these economies (e.g., Indonesia, the Philippines) will nevertheless reduce their gap with the advanced economies during the rest of this century because they grow faster, but they will not reach the income per capita levels of the advanced economies. Some other countries in this group in South Asia, Southeast Asia, and Central Asia, as well as in the Pacific, are much farther behind on all four areas considered in this book. For them, development will continue being a very slow process during the rest of the 21st century.

References

Acemoglu, Daron, and Fabrizio Zilibotti. 1999. "Information Accumulation in Development." *Journal of Economic Growth* 4(1): 5–38.
Acemoglu, Daron, and Pascual Restrepo. 2018. "Demographics and Automation." NBER Working Paper No. 24421. Cambridge, MA: National Bureau of Economic Research.
Acemoglu, Daron, and Pascual Restrepo. 2019. "Automation and New Tasks: How Technology Displaces and Reinstates Labor." *Journal of Economic Perspectives* 33(2): 3–30.
Amsden, Alice H. 1989. *Asia's Next Giant: South Korea and Late Industrialization.* New York and Oxford: Oxford University Press.
Amsden, Alice H. 1994. "Why Isn't the Whole World Experimenting with the East Asian Model to Develop?: Review of the East Asian Miracle." *World Development* 22(4): 627–33.
Amsden, Alice H. 1995. "Like the Rest: South-East Asia's 'LATE' Industrialization." *Journal of International Development* 7(5): 791–9.
Ang, James B., and Jakob B. Madsen. 2011. "Can Second-Generation Endogenous Growth Models Explain the Productivity Trends and Knowledge Production in the Asian Miracle Economies?" *The Review of Economics and Statistics* 93(4): 1360–73.
Asian Development Bank. 2013. "Asia's Economic Transformation: Where to, How, and How Fast? Key Indicators for Asia and the Pacific 2013." Special Chapter. Manila: Asian Development Bank.
Autor, David, David Dorn, and Gordon Hanson. 2013. "The China Syndrome: Local Labor Market Effects of Import Competition in the United States." *American Economic Review*, 103(6): 2121–68.
Baldwin, Richard. 2011. "Trade and Industrialisation After Globalisation's 2nd Unbundling: How Building and Joining a Supply Chain Are Different and Why It Matters." NBER Working Paper No. 17716. Cambridge, MA: National Bureau of Economic Research.
Bell, Martin, and Keith Pavitt. 1995. "The Development of Technological Capabilities." In *Trade, Technology, and International Competitiveness*, edited by I. U. Haque, 69–101. Washington, D.C.: World Bank
Bernhofen, Daniel M., Zouheir El-Sahli, and Richard Kneller. 2016. "Estimating the Effects of the Container Revolution on World Trade." *Journal of International Economics* 98: 36–50.

References

Chenery, Hollis B., and Lance Taylor. 1968. "Development Patterns: Among Countries and Over Time." *Review of Economics and Statistics* 50(4): 391–416.

Cimoli, Mario, Giovanni Dosi, and Joseph E. Stiglitz. (eds.) 2009. *Industrial Policy and Development: The Political Economy of Capabilities Accumulation*. Oxford, UK: Oxford University Press.

Dachs, Bernhard, and Stefan Pahl. 2019. "Are Global Value Chains in Decline?" London, UK: London School of Economics and Political Science. https://blogstest.lse.ac.uk/gild/2019/07/26/are-global-value-chains-in-decline/.

Das, Mitali, and Bejamin Hilgenstock. 2022. "The Exposure to Routinization: Labor Market Implications for Developed and Developing Economies." *Structural Change and Economic Dynamics* 60: 99–113.

Dollar, David. 2019. "How Global Value Chains Open Opportunities for Developing Countries." Brookings. https://www.brookings.edu/articles/how-global-value-chains-open-opportunities-for-developing-countries/.

Dosi, Giovanni, Andrea Roventini, and Emanuele Russo. 2020. "Public Policies and the Art of Catching Up: Matching the Historical Evidence with a Multicountry Agent-Based Model." *Industrial and Corporate Change* 30: 1011–36. https://doi.org/10.1093/icc/dtaa057.

Elia, Stefano, Luciano Fratocchi, Paolo Barbieri, Albachiara Boffellid, and Matteo Kalchschmidt. 2021. "Post-Pandemic Reconfiguration from Global to Domestic and Regional Value Chains: The Role of Industrial Policies." *Transnational Corporations* 28(2): 67–96.

European Patent Office. 2020. "Patents and the Fourth Industrial Revolution. The Global Technology Trends Enabling the Data-Driven Economy." https://link.epo.org/web/fourth_industrial_revolution_2017__en.pdf.

Felipe, Jesus, and John S. L. McCombie. 2003. "Some Methodological Problems with the Neoclassical Analysis of the East Asian Miracle." *Cambridge Journal of Economics* 54(5): 695–721.

Felipe, Jesus, Utsav Kumar, Arnelyn Abdon, and Marife Bacate. 2012. "Product Complexity and Economic Development." *Structural Change and Economic Dynamics* 23(1): 36–68.

Felipe, Jesus, and Aashish Mehta. 2016. "Deindustrialization? A Global Perspective." *Economics Letters* 149: 148–51.

Felipe, Jesus, Connie Bayudan-Dacuycuy, and Matteo Lanzafame. 2016. "The Declining Share of Agricultural Employment in China: How Fast?" *Structural Change and Economic Dynamics* 37: 127–37.

Felipe, Jesus, Aashish Mehta, and Changyong Rhee. 2019. "Manufacturing Matters…But It's the Jobs That Count." *Cambridge Journal of Economics* 43: 139–68.

Felipe, J., Matteo Lanzafame, and Gemma Estrada. 2019. "Is Indonesia's Growth Rate Balance-of-Payments-Constrained? A Time-Varying Estimation Approach." *Review of Keynesian Economics* 7(4): 537–53.

Felipe, J., and Matteo Lanzafame. 2020. "The PRC's Long-Run Growth through the Lens of the Export-Led Growth Model." *Journal of Comparative Economics* 48: 163–181.

Felipe, Jesus, John S. L. McCombie, and Aashish Mehta. 2025. "Is Anything Left of the Debate about the Sources of Growth in East Asia Thirty Years Later? A Critical Survey." *Journal of Evolutionary Economics*. https://doi.org/10.1007/s00191-025-00894-w.

References

Foster-McGregor, Neil, Önder Nomaler, and Bart Verspagen. 2019. "Measuring the Creation and Adoption of New Technologies Using Trade and Patent Data." MERIT Working Papers 2019-053. Maastricht, Netherlands: United Nations University – Maastricht Economic and Social Research Institute on Innovation and Technology (MERIT).

Foster-McGregor, Neil, Ludovico Alcorta, Adam Szirmai, and Bart Verspagen. 2021. *New Perspectives on Structural Change: Causes and Consequences of Structural Change in the Global Economy*. Oxford, UK: Oxford University Press.

Foster-McGregor, Neil, Önder Nomaler, and Bart Verspagen. 2024a. "The Innovation and Structural Transformation Database." DataverseNL, V1. https://doi.org/10.34894/LQZLBP.

Foster-McGregor, Neil, Önder Nomaler, and Bart Verspagen. 2024b. "The Innovation and Structural Transformation Database: A Guide." MERIT Working Papers 2024-027. Maastricht, Netherlands: United Nations University – Maastricht Economic and Social Research Institute on Innovation and Technology (MERIT).

Freeman, Christopher. 1988. "Technology Gaps, International Trade, and the Problems of Smaller and Less-Developed Economies." In *Small Countries Facing the Technological Revolution*, edited by C. Freeman, and B. Å. Lundvall, 67–85. London: Pinter Publishers.

Fu, Xiaolan, and Liu Shi. 2022. "Direction of Innovation in Developing Countries and Its Driving Forces." Economic Research Working Paper No. 69. Geneva, Switzerland: World Intellectual Property Organization (WIPRO).

Gerschenkron, Alexander. 1962. *Economic Backwardness in Historical Perspective*. Cambridge, MA, USA: Harvard University Press.

Giglioli, Simona, Giorgia Giovannetti, Enrico Marvasi, and Arianna Vivoli. 2021. "The Resilience of Global Value Chains During the COVID-19 Pandemic: The Case of Italy." Working Papers No. wp2021/07. Florence, Italy: Universita' degli Studi di Firenze.

Grossman, Gene M., and Elhanan Helpman. 1991. *Innovation and Growth in the Global Economy*. Cambridge, MA, USA: The MIT Press.

Hausmann, Ricardo, Jason Hwang, and Dani Rodrik. 2007. "What You Export Matters." *Journal of Economic Growth* 12: 1–25.

Hausmann, Ricardo, César A. Hidalgo, Sebastián Bustos, Michele Coscia, Sarah Chung, Juan Jimenez, Alexander Simoes, and Muhammed Ali Yildirim. 2014. *The Atlas of Economic Complexity: Mapping Paths to Prosperity*. Cambridge, MA, USA: The MIT Press.

Hidalgo, César A., Bailey Klinger, A.-L. Barabási, and Ricardo Hausmann. 2007. "The Product Space Conditions the Development of Nations." *Science* 317(5837): 482–7.

Hidalgo, César A., and Ricardo Hausmann. 2009. "The Building Blocks of Economic Complexity." *Proceedings of the National Academy of Sciences* 106(26): 10570–75.

Hobday, Michael. 1995a. *Innovation in East Asia. The Challenge to Japan*. Cheltenham, UK: Edward Elgar.

Hobday, Michael. 1995b. "East Asian Latecomer Firms: Learning the Technology of Electronics." *World Development* 23(7): 1171–93.

Johnson, Chalmers. 1982. *MITI and the Japanese Miracle*. Stanford: Stanford University Press.

Jomo, Kwame Sundaram, and Tan Kok Wah. (eds.) 1999. *Industrial Policy in East Asia. Lessons for Malaysia*. Kuala Lumpur, Malaysia: University of Malaya Press.

References

Juhász, Réka, Nathan Lane, and Dani Rodrik. 2023. "The New Economics of Industrial Policy." Working Paper No. 31538. Cambridge, MA, USA: National Bureau of Economic Research. https://www.nber.org/papers/w31538

Kaldor, Nicholas. 1967. *Strategic Factors in Economic Development*. Ithaca, New York: Cornell University Press.

Kee, Hiau Looi, and Heiwai Tang. 2016. "Domestic Value Added in Exports: Theory and Firm Evidence from China." *American Economic Review* 106(6): 1402–36.

Khan, Mushtaq H. 2015. "Industrial Policy Design and Implementation Challenges." In *Development and Modern Industrial Policy in Practice: Issues and Country Experiences*. Cheltenham, UK: Asian Development Bank and Edward Elgar Publishing. https://doi.org/10.4337/9781784715540.

Kim, Linsu. 1997. *From Imitation to Innovation: Dynamics of Korea's Technological Learning*. Boston, MA, USA: Harvard Business School Press.

Kim, Jong Il, and Lawrence J. Lau. 1994. "The Sources of Economic Growth of the East Asian Newly Industrialized Countries." *Journal of the Japanese and International Economies* 8(3): 235–71.

Kojima, Koji. 2000. "The "Flying Geese" Model of Asian Economic Development: Origin, Theoretical Extensions, and Regional Policy Implications." *Journal of Asian Economics* 11(4): 375–401.

Koopman, Robert, Zhi Wang, and Shang-Jin Wei. 2014. "Tracing Value-Added and Double Counting in Gross Exports." *American Economic Review* 104(2): 459–94.

Kremer, Michael. 1993. "The O-Ring Theory of Economic Development." *The Quarterly Journal of Economics* 108(3): 551–75.

Krueger, Anne O. 1998. "Why Trade Liberalisation Is Good for Growth." *Economic Journal* 108(450): 1513–52.

Kuznets, Simon. 1966. *Modern Economic Growth*. New Haven, CT, USA: Yale University Press.

Kwon, Jene. 1994. "The East Asia Challenge to Neoclassical Orthodoxy." *World Development* 22(4): 635–44.

Lall, Sanjaya. 1992. "Technological Capabilities and Industrialization." *World Development* 20(2): 165–86.

Lall, Sanjaya. 2000. "The Technological Structure and Performance of Developing Country Manufactured Exports, 1985–1998." Queen Elizabeth House Working Paper No. 44. Oxford, UK: University of Oxford.

Lane, Nathan. 2022. "Manufacturing Revolutions: Industrial Policy and Industrialization in South Korea." CSAE Working Paper Series. https://doi.org/10.2139/ssrn.3890311.

Lee, Keun. 2024. "Economics of Technology Cycle Time (TCT) and Catch-Up by Latecomers: Micro-, Meso-, and Macro-Analyses and Implications." *Journal of Evolutionary Economics* 34: 319–49. https://doi.org/10.1007/s00191-024-00847-9.

Lee, Keun, and John A. Mathews. 2012. "South Korea and Taiwan." In *Innovative Firms in Emerging Market Economies*, edited by J. Cantwell and E. Amann, 223–45.

Legendre, Pierre, and Louis Legendre. 1998. *Numerical Ecology*. 2nd ed. Amsterdam: Elsevier Science.

Malerba, Franco, and Keun Lee. 2021. "An Evolutionary Perspective on Economic Catch-Up by Latecomers." *Industrial and Corporate Change* 30(4): 986–1010.

Mealy, Penny, J. Doyne Farmer, and Alexander Teytelboym. 2019. "Interpreting Economic Complexity." *Science Advances* 5: eaau1705. https://doi.org/10.1126/sciadv.aau1705.

References

Melitz, Marc J. 2003. "The Impact of Trade on Intra-Industry Reallocations and Aggregate Industry Productivity." *Econometrica* 71(6): 1695–725.

Menéndez de Medina, Maria, Önder Nomaler, and Bart Verspagen. 2023. "Identification of Fourth Industrial Revolution Technologies Using PATSTAT Data." UNU-MERIT Working Papers 2023–023.

Nelson, Richard, and Howard, Pack. 1999. "The Asian Growth Miracle and Modern Growth Theory." *Economic Journal* 109(457): 416–36.

Nomaler, Önder, and Bart Verspagen. 2024. "Reinterpreting Economic Complexity in Multiple Dimensions." https://doi.org/10.48550/arXiv.2409.01830.

Pack, Howard, and Kamal Saggi. 2006. "Is There a Case for Industrial Policy? A Critical Survey." *The World Bank Research Observer* 21(2): 267–97.

Perez, Carlota, and Luc Soete. 1988. "Catching Up in Technology: Entry Barriers and Windows of Opportunity." In *Technical Change and Economic Theory*, edited by G. Dosi, R. R. Freeman, R. Nelson, G. Silverberg, and L. Soete, 459–79. London: Pinter Publishers.

Rodrik, Dani, Xinshen Diao, and Margaret McMillan. 2017. "The Recent Growth Boom in Developing Economies: A Structural-Change Perspective." In *The Palgrave Handbook of Development Economics*, 281–334. London, UK: Palgrave Macmillan. https://drodrik.scholar.harvard.edu/publications/recent-growth-boom-developing-economies-structural-change-perspective.

Romer, Paul, M. 1990. "Endogenous Technological Change." *Journal of Political Economy* 98 (5), S71–S102.

Saviotti, Pier Paolo, and Andreas Pyka. 2011. "Generalized Barriers to Entry and Economic Development." *Journal of Evolutionary Economics* 21: 29–52. https://doi.org/10.1007/s00191-010-0184-2.

Stapleton, Katherine. 2019. "Automation, Global Value Chains and Development: What Do We Know So Far?" Pathways for Prosperity Commission Background Paper Series No. 26.

Stiglitz, Joseph E. 1996. "Some Lessons from the East Asian Miracle." *The World Bank Research Observer* 11(2): 151–77.

Studwell, Joe. 2013. *How Asia Works: Success and Failure in the World's Most Dynamic Region*. New York, NY, USA: Grove Press.

Sutton, John. 2001. "Rich Trades, Scarce Capabilities: Industrial Development Revisited." Keynes Lecture, British Academy 2000. Proceedings of the British Academy, London, UK.

Sutton, John. 2005. "Competing in Capabilities: An Informal Overview." Manuscript. London, UK: London School of Economics.

Szirmai, Adam. 2012. "Industrialisation as an Engine of Growth in Developing Countries, 1950–2005." *Structural Change and Economic Dynamics* 23(4): 406–20.

Szirmai, Adam, and Bart Verspagen. 2015. "Manufacturing and Economic Growth in Developing Countries, 1950–2005." *Structural Change and Economic Dynamics* 34: 46–59.

Taglioni, Daria, and Deborah Winkler. 2016. "*Making Global Value Chains Work for Development*." Washington, DC, USA: World Bank.

Thirlwall, Anthony Philip. 1979. "The Balance of Payments Constraint as an Explanation of International Growth Rate Differences." *Banca Nazionale del Laboro Quarterly Review* 32(128): 45–53.

Timmer, Marcel P., Bart Los, Robert Stehrer, and Gaaitzen J. de Vries. 2021. "Supply Chain Fragmentation and the Global Trade Elasticity: A New Accounting Framework." *IMF Economic Review* 69: 656–80.

Van Dam, Alje, Mark Dekker, Ignacio Morales-Castilla, Miguel Á. Rodríguez, David Wichmann, and Mara Baudena. 2021. "Correspondence Analysis, Spectral Clustering and Graph Embedding: Applications to Ecology and Economic Complexity." *Scientific Reports* 11: 8926. https://doi.org/10.1038/s41598-021-87971-9.

Wade, Robert. 1990. *Governing the Market: Economic Theory and the Role of Government in East Asian Industrialization*. Princeton: Princeton University Press.

World Bank. 1993. *The East Asian Miracle. Economic Growth and Public Policy*. Washington, DC, USA: World Bank.

World Bank, and World Trade Organization. 2019. *Global Value Chain Development Report 2019: Technical Innovation, Supply Chain Trade, and Workers in a Globalized World*. Washington, D.C.: World Bank Group.

World Trade Organization. 2021. *Global Value Chain Development Report: Beyond Production*. World Trade Organization. Asian Development Bank, Research Institute for Global Value Chains at the University of International Business and Economics, the World Trade Organization, the Institute of Developing Economies – Japan External Trade Organization, and the China Development Research Foundation.

World Trade Organization. 2023. *Global Value Chain Development Report: Resilient and Sustainable GVCs in Turbulent Times*. World Trade Organization. Research Institute for Global Value Chains at the University of International Business and Economics, Asian Development Bank, the Institute of Developing Economies – Japan External Trade Organization and the World Trade Organization.

Young, Alwyn. 1992. "A Tale of Two Cities: Factor Accumulation and Technical Change in Hong Kong and Singapore." *NBER Macroeconomics Annual* 7: 13–54.

Young, Alwyn. 1994. "Lessons from the East Asian NICs: A Contrarian View." *European Economic Review* 38(3–4): 964–73.

Young, Alwyn. 1995. "The Tyranny of the Numbers: Confronting the Statistical Realities of the East Asian Growth Experience." *Quarterly Journal of Economics* 110(3): 641–80.

Zhan, James, Richard Bolwijn, Bruno Casella, and Amelia U Santos-Paulino. 2020. "Global Value Chain Transformation to 2030: Overall Direction and Policy Implications." VoxEU.org. https://voxeu.org/article/global-value-chain-transformation-decade-ahead.

Index

Note: Italicized page references refer to figures, **bold** references refer to tables, and page references with "n" refer to endnotes.

Acemoglu, D. 26n1, 81
additive manufacturing 6, 22, 79;
　see also Fourth Industrial Revolution (4IR)
Afghanistan 1, 28
Amsden, Alice H. 16, 23–25
Ang, James B. 26n3
Armenia 1
artificial intelligence (AI) 6, 22, 79
Asian Development Bank 18, 39n1, 43;
　multi-country input output tables 4
Asian economies 1–6, 28–29, 48, 85–86, 91; complexity of foreign and domestic intermediates of 70–72; Fourth Industrial Revolution (4IR) 79–89, 92–93; output complexity of electricals and textiles 72–74; performance in terms of GVC integration 54; period 2000–2019 of 34; production activities of 68–70; productivity growth across 34; in terms of 4IR patenting RTA 84; and USA and Germany 84
Azerbaijan 1

backward integration 4, 8, 47, 49–50, 52–53, 55–56, 72, 74, 91, 92
backward linkages 43, 45–50, *50*, 60
backward radius 52, *52*, 53, *54*, 57, *57*, *58*, 59, *59*
balance-of-payments-constrained (BOPC) 25–26
Baldwin, Richard 41
Bangladesh 1, 3, 17, 32, 41, 49, 52–53, 68, 70, 74, 76

Bell, Martin 26n1
Bhutan 1, 52, 70–72, 74, 76
Broad Economic Categories (BEC) 66, 78n2
Brunei Darussalam 1, 28, 47, 52–53, 72, 74, 76–77

Cambodia 1, 3, 24, 28, 32, 48, 50, 52, 67, 68, 70–72, 74
capabilities 2–3, 16–18, 27, 49, 63–64, 68, 70, 72, 74, 90, 93–94; accumulation of 18–22; domestic production 42, 49, 60; importance of 26n1; organizational 20; product-specific 63; sophistication/uniqueness 62; technical 20
capital 16, 44; goods **9**, **10**, 80, 83, 94; growth 2; human 19, 20; intellectual 80; intensity 39; physical 19
catch-up institutions, Singapore and Taiwan 24
China 2–4, 6, 17, 19, 26, 32, 41–42, 46–47, 49–51, 53, 74, 77, 82–85, 89n3; 4IR production and use 86–89; backward integration 55, *55*; change in employment shares *38*; change in relative labor productivity *36*; developments in productivity performance 34–39; divergent trends 54–59; GVC integration for 54, *55*, *56*, 60–61, 91; initial employment shares *36*; labor productivity growth and components *35*; sectoral labor productivity *38*; within-sector productivity growth effect *36*

Index

Cimoli, Mario 23
comparative advantage 6, 19, 23, 40, 63–65, 93
complexity 64; comparative advantage of product 65; concept of 19; and development 65; of electricals production 70, 72–74, 73, 75, 76; final output 76–77; foreign/domestic input 67, 68, 68–70, 69; of foreign/domestic intermediates 70–72; foreign intermediate inputs 74–76; GVC-complexity variables 66; indicators 62; of inputs/output 62–63, 92; literatures 19, 21; as measure of upgrading 63–66; of products 8, 62–66; in textiles 70, 72–74, 73, 75; values 65; *see also* economic complexity; input complexity

DB_GVC_Integration.xlsx 8, **14**, 43
DB_GVC_Radius.xlsx 8, **15**
DB_Input_And_Output_Complexities. xlsx. 8, **13**, 63
DB_IR4patents_2000_2019.xlsx 8, **13–14**
DB_Patents_Embedded_in_GVCs.xlsx 8, **14**
DB_Structural_Change_Basic_ Indicators.xlsx 7, **9**, 80
DB_Structural_Change_ ProductivityGrowth.xlsx 7, **12**, 28
DB_Upgrading_Capabilities.xlsx 8, **13**
developing countries 18–19, 23, 25, 41, 60
development 26n1, 26n2; Asian economies 1, 2–3, 16–26, 90–94; and complexity 62–63, 65; deindustrialization 28; in Global Value Chains 40–61; labor productivity 27–28; in productivity performance 34–39; structural change 30
developmental state model 23–24
diversification **13**, 18, 60
Dosi, Giovanni 22
dynamic structural transformation 3, **12**, 25, 28, 30–33, *34*, 34–35, 91

East Asia 16, 23; firms 22; growth/ development 2, 17, 18–19; latecomer model and government intervention 23–24; role of industrial policy in 23; success in 1960s–1980s 18–22
economic complexity 1; in GVCs 5, 62–77; *see also* complexity

economic policy 61
electricals sector 5, 67–77, 92
electronics 21–23, 41
employment: agricultural share decline in East Asia 18–19; in agriculture, manufacturing, and services 19, 30–34; change in structure of **12–13**, 27–28, 30–31, 33–34, 36–39; contribution to structural transformation 18–22, 30–34; data indicators (employment index, share) **12–13**; decomposition by sector 30–31, *31*, 33, 35; initial sectoral shares (China, Vietnam) 33, 36–39; manufacturing share trends 18–19; movement toward dynamic sectors 28; reallocation across sectors 30, 34, 40; shifts in, role in economic development 18; structural change effect 30–34; within-sector effects 30–34, 35, *36*; *see also* labor productivity
export 2–5, **9–12**, **15**, 18–21, 24–25, 40, 49, 51–52, 60, 80–81, 83, 89; in 4IR technologies 6, *84*, 84–87, *88*, 89n2; comparative advantage in 63; complexity of 62; GVCs 8, *51*; structure of 7, 17

Felipe, Jesus 2–3, 16, 18–19, 26, 26n3, 63
Fiji 1, 52, 53
forward integration 45, 46, 48–50, 53, 56, 91
forward linkages 47–49, 56, 91
forward radius 52, 53, *53*, *54*, 57, *58*, 59
Foster-McGregor, Neil 7, 45, 66, 81
Fourth Industrial Revolution (4IR) **13–14**, 79–89; characteristics and definition 6, 79–80; country comparisons 86–90; development disparities across Asia 6, 92–93; economic impact and inequality 6, 80, 92–93; engagement metrics 80; innovation and patenting 81–83; product trade patterns 83–85; regional specialization and integration 86–89, 90–93; role in development analysis 6–7, 90–91; *see also* technology/technological

General-Purpose Technologies 6, 22, 79
Georgia 1, 3, 32

Index 103

Gerschenkron, Alexander 23–24
Global Value Chains (GVCs) 3–7, 8; challenges and criticisms 41–42, 60; complexity measures and innovation 65–68; and development 59–61; as development paradigm 40–43; divergent trends (China and Vietnam) 54–59; evolution of 59–61; geographical shifts and regionalization 52–54; integration 4–5, 8, **14–15**, 22, 41–51, 52–56, *55, 56, 57,* 60, 62–63, 72, 74–77, 91, 92; policy implications and industrial strategy 42, 60, 91; positioning 43–51; radius 52, 53, 57

Hausmann, Ricardo 19, 63, 65
Hidalgo, César A. 19, 63, 65
Hobday, Michael 22
Hong Kong 1–2, 16–17, 21–22, 24–25, 28, 47–49, 52–53, 78, 82–83, 93; developmental experience and policy context 24–25; GVC participation 49, 52–53; as part of East Asian development model 1–2, 16–17, 19, 21–22; technology and innovation 82–83

import 7, **9–12, 15**, 25, 85; of 4IR technologies 6, 80, 83, *85,* 86, *89,* 93; of non-durable consumer goods 17; restrictions 17; substitution 17, 40
import-substitution policy 17
India 1–2, 17, 24, 26n5, 43–49, 53, 66, 71–72, 74, 82, 85
indicators 1, 7, **9–15**, 28, 43, 53, 59, 61, 63, 65, 66; backward integration 49, 74; GVC 4, 5, 8, 45–46, 62; novel 52; RTA 81; upgrading **13**
Indonesia 1, 3, 7, 17, 19, 24–26, 34, 48–50, 67, 71, 74
industrial catch-up 18, 21, 24
industrialization 4, 17–18, 20, 22, 24–25, 27–28, 40–41
industrial policy 3, 17, 18, 22–25; arguments for and against 22–25; capability building and technological upgrading, 6, 21–22; historical evolution and theory 22–24; recent reevaluation 25; relation to balance-of-payments constraints 18
innovation 8, 80; incentive for 40; national innovation systems 21;
opportunities 42; role of capabilities 26n1
input complexity: foreign and domestic *67,* 67–68, *68, 69,* 70–76, *71, 73, 75;* foreign intermediate inputs 74–76; *see also* complexity
intermediates: complex 68; deliveries 66; domestic 70–72; foreign 70–72, 74–76, 92; goods **9, 13,** 44, 46, 53, 62, 66; innovations 6; production 70; suppliers in GVCs 48; in total exports/imports **9–10**

Japan 1–2, 6, 16, 24–25, 28, 47, 51, 53, 66, 68, 70, 72, 74, 77, 83–84, 86–87
Johnson, Chalmers 23
Jomo, Kwame Sundaram 23
Juhász, Réka 25

Kazakhstan 1, 47, 49, 51, 70, 74, 77
Khan, Mushtaq H. 20
Kim, Linsu 22
Koopman, Robert 45
Kremer, Michael 26n1
Kwon, Jene 16
Kyrgyz Republic 1, 47, 71, 76

labor productivity 7; change in relative *36;* contribution in manufacturing 3, 28–30, *29,* 34–39; growth and components *35;* sectoral *38;* and structural change 3, 7, 28; and structural transformation 27–39
Lall, Sanjaya 26n1, 64–65
Lall classification scheme 64–65
Lane, Nathan 25
Lanzafame, Matteo 26
Lao PDR 1, 3, 32, 52, 67, 70–72, 74, 77, 84
latecomer model 23–24, 26n2
learning-by-doing (LBD) 20
Legendre, Louis 64
Legendre, Pierre 64
linkages: backward 43, 45–50, *50,* 60; forward 47–49, 56, 91

Madsen, Jakob B. 26n3
Malaysia 1, 7, 17, 24–25, 47–48, 51–53, 66, 71, 77, 82, 84, 85, 94
Maldives 1, 47, 48, 53
manufacturing: additive 6, 22; contribution to labor productivity growth 28–30, *29,* 34–39;

as driver of structural transformation 18–22; importance of 18, 27; labor productivity 3; low-tech goods 49, 59; in recent years 4; shares of employment and value-added in 28
McCombie, John S. L. 2, 16
Mehta, Aashish 19
Menéndez de Medina, Maria 81
Mongolia 1, 47, 52, 70, 72, 74, 76, 77
Myanmar 1, 3, 28, 32

Nepal 1, 28, 47, 48–50, 52, 70, 72, 74, 76
Nomaler, Önder 64

Pack, Howard 22, 26n5
Pakistan 1, 17, 47–51, 53, 67, 70–72, 77
Papua New Guinea 1, 3, 32
patents 6; 4IR technologies 8, 80, 81–83, 84, 86–87; family 8, **13–14**, 89n1, 89n4
Pavitt, Keith 26n1
Perez, Carlota 20
personal-digital assistants (PDAs) 79
Philippines 1, 2, 7, 17, 19, 48–49, 68, 70, 72, 74, 77, 82, 84–85, 94
policy: China+1 61; debates 27; economic 61; import-substitution 17; interventions 60; "Made in China 2025" 61; *see also* industrial policy
product complexity 7, 8, 63–66
product complexity index (PCI) 63–64
productivity: decomposition **12–13**, 30–33; growth 2, 3–4, 7, 16, 18, 22, 28–34; performance 34–39; relative sectoral 28; within-sector 3, 18, 28, 30–34, 35, *36*, 39, 90; *see also* labor productivity

quality-productivity combinations 20

radius: backward 52, *52*, 53, *54*, 57, *57*, *58*, 59, *59*; forward 52, 53, *53*, *54*, 57, *58*, 59; GVC 52, 53
relative sectoral productivity 28
Restrepo, P. 81
Revealed Comparative Advantage (RCA) **9–12**, 64, 81, *88*, *89*, 89n2
Revealed Technological Advantage (RTA) 81–84, *82*, 86–87, *88*, 89, 89n2
robots 87, 89
Rodrik, Dani 18
RTA indicator 81

Saggi, Kamal 22, 26n5
Samoa 1
Schumpeterian model 20–21, 26n3
Second Industrial Revolution 5
Singapore 1–2, 6, 16–17, 19, 21–22, 24–25, 28, 47–50, 52–53, 70, 72–73, 82–83
smile curve concept 49
Soete, Luc 20
Solomon Islands 1, 32
South Korea 1–2, 6, 16, 17, 18, 19, 21–22, 24–25, 26n4, 28, 40, 47, 50, 53, 74
Sri Lanka 1, 47–48, 50, 53, 70, 77, 82
static structural transformation 3, **12**, 30, 32–33, *33*, 35, 91
Stiglitz, Joseph E. 16, 23
structural change: data sources and structural transformation database 7, **9–12**; definition and decomposition 3–4, 27, 30–31; drivers of productivity growth 3–4, 27–35; effects (shift-share method) 30–31, *34*, 35; and employment 30; and labor productivity 3, 7, 28; sectoral analysis and employment shifts 3, 32–34, 39
structural transformation 17; and accumulation of capabilities 18–22; analysis of 22; defined 3; indicators of 6; and labor productivity 27–39; Malaysia and Thailand 7
Studwell, Joe 40
Sutton, John 20
Szirmai, Adam 18

Taiwan 1, 2, 6, 16–19, 21, 22, 24–25, 49, 51–52, 70, 72, 74, 83–85, 93
Tajikistan 1
technology/technological 5–7, 20–21; 3D printing **10**, **11**, **12**; automation 42; CADCAM **10**, **11**; digital 3, 79–81; ICT **10**, **11**; indicators 8; leaders 26n2; learning 22; measure of 20; progress and long-run growth 40; Regulating Instruments **10**, **11**; revolutions 92; Robot **10**, **11**, **12**; sophistication of sectors 39; subfields 86–87, *88*, 89n4; Welding **10**, **11**, **12**; *see also* Fourth Industrial Revolution (4IR)
textiles/textile products sector 5, 17, 24, 63, 65, 66–77, 92

Index 105

Thailand 1, 6, 7, 17, 24–25, 47, 48, 50, 74, 77, 85
Thirlwall, Anthony Philip 25
Timmer, Marcel P. 45
Timor-Leste 1, 32
Tonga 1
trade: in 4IR products 83–85; agreements 54; between China and USA 61; and GVCs 22, 42; international 7–8, 40; literature 81; openness 46; rapid liberalization of 41; role in transforming economies 40
Turkmenistan 1

upgrading 18, 41, 70, 72–74, 92; complexity 5, 63–66; importance of 41; indicators **13**; industrial 20; issues of 42; opportunities 5, 8, 41, 49; possibilities 8; structural 17; structural transformation cum 25; substantial 3
Uzbekistan 1

value-added: activities 42, 49; exports 51; shares in manufacturing 28; share *vs.* change 75, *76*, *77*; of value chains 41
Vanuatu 1
Verspagen, Bart 18, 64
Vietnam 1–4, 17, 32, 34–39, 41–42, 47–52, 54–59, 60–61, 68, 72, 74, 77, 82, 84–85, 90

Wade, Robert 16, 23
Wah, Tan Kok 23
within-sector productivity 3, 18, 28, 30–34, 35, *36*, 39, 90
World Bank 16, 22, 41–42

Young, Alwyn 16, 22

Zhan, James 91
Zillibotti, F. 26n1
z-Score 78n1

Printed in the United States
by Baker & Taylor Publisher Services